THE

A GUIDE FOR FIRST TIME LEADERS TO
DEVELOP LEADERSHIP COMPETENCIES

FIRST

AND EMBRACE THEIR UNIQUE
LEADERSHIP JOURNEY

ONE

MARIA ASUELIMEN

WESTBOW
PRESS®
A DIVISION OF THOMAS NELSON
& ZONDERVAN

WestBow Press books may be ordered through booksellers or by contacting:

WestBow Press
A Division of Thomas Nelson & Zondervan
1663 Liberty Drive
Bloomington, IN 47403
www.westbowpress.com
844-714-3454

ISBN: 979-8-3850-1798-0 (sc)
ISBN: 979-8-3850-1799-7 (hc)
ISBN: 979-8-3850-1800-0 (e)

Library of Congress Control Number: 2024901987

Print information available on the last page.

WestBow Press rev. date: 02/28/2024

CONTENTS

Dedication ix

Introduction xi

Part I. Leading Yourself

Chapter 1   Identity: Who Are You? 1

    Confusion 12

    Control 13

    Insecurity 15

    Underperformance 17

Chapter 2   What Is the Size of Your Cup? 20

    Capacity 20

    Intuition 23

    Leadership Presence 28

    Character 29

    Confidence 30

    Charisma and Oratory Prowess 31

    Tenacity 33

    Domain Expertise 40

Chapter 3   Leadership Philosophy 51

Chapter 4   WHAT DO YOU WANT TO DO? 58

    Vision 58

    Assignment 62

    Goals 65

Part II. Leading People

Chapter 5   Leaders Need People.. 69
             Who Are Your People?... 72
             Your People Need What You Have.................................74
             Your People Generally Share the Same Values as You.......... 78
             Your People Are Those Who Have the Capacity to Get
             the Job Done.. 92
             Knowledge... 94
             Skills... 96
             Talent and Ability 99
             Reciprocity: What Makes People Loyal? 100

Chapter 6   Relationship Management.. 104
             Building Trust... 106
             Defining and Categorizing Relationships.................... 108
             Team Members 108
             Partners 110
             Colleagues 112
             Acquaintances...113
             Stakeholders 114
             Public Followers 116
             Terminating/Changing Relationships 117
             Avoiding Toxic Relationships 117

Part III. Leading in an Organization

Chapter 7   Navigating an Organization's Dynamics 125
             Organizational Culture 128
             Be Solution-Oriented.. 139

Chapter 8   Driving Organizational Performance............................ 143
             Managing Resources.. 151
             Group Norms and Social Influence.............................167
             Unrealistic Timelines 169

Chapter 9 Crisis Management...171
            Affair and Allegations 177
            Conclusion 179
            Tips to Increase Competencies of Leading Yourself.............. 180
            Tips to Increase Competencies on Leading People 182
            Tips to Increasing Competencies on Leading an
            Organization.. 184

DEDICATION

This book is dedicated to my father Late Chief Dr. William Oku Ekeruche. The man who made me secure in my identity and who taught me the value of knowledge. Daddy although you never got to read this book, It is a testament of your legacy as a champion of education and an avid supporter of women leaders. Daddy because you raised me as a human being and not just a woman, I am who I am today. This first one is for you.

INTRODUCTION

In the movie, *Frozen,* Elsa is the older sister of Princess Anna and the heir to the throne of Arendelle. From a young age, Elsa possesses the power to control ice and snow. However, she struggles to control her abilities, and after accidentally injuring her younger sister, she becomes fearful of hurting others.

To protect herself and those around her, Elsa isolates herself from the world, living in fear of her powers and suppressing her emotions. She builds an ice palace high in the mountains and hides away from the kingdom.

As the story unfolds, Elsa's fears escalate, leading her to accidentally plunge Arendelle into an eternal winter during her coronation as queen. This incident forces Elsa to confront her powers and her fears. With the help and love of Anna, along with other friends, Elsa begins to understand that her abilities are not a curse but a part of who she is.

Through a journey of self-discovery and acceptance, Elsa learns to embrace her powers and control them. She realizes that love, not fear, is the key to managing her abilities. In the end, Elsa saves Arendelle and her sister by harnessing her powers for the greater good.

Elsa's journey in *Frozen* is about discovering her true self and accepting her magical abilities. We all have magical abilities that we need to define, accept, cultivate, and put to good use. Like Elsa, our magic is needed in this world generally, and in the space where we currently exist. Leadership is the act of uncovering our magic and the magic in others and putting For some years now, I have settled on the concept of magnificent leadership. The word "magnificence" comes from the Latin phrase magnum facere, which means "to do something great." I define "magnificent leadership" as using your inner light to light the path of others to accomplish great things. It involves constantly keeping your inner light on, shining it on the path of your team that comes alongside you to accomplish something great for good.

Magnificent leadership is about taking people with diverse backgrounds and expertise on a journey toward a future that is different from what they currently have, with more possibilities and positive outcomes. A grand future! This type of leadership requires distinct skills, abilities, and knowledge, depending on your industry, the composition of your team members, your position in the business organization, and other factors.

People are drawn to leaders because the widely accepted narrative of leadership depicts power and control; charisma and influence; affluence and fame. People admire leaders because of their perceived license to tell others what to do and control their own time. They relish the idea of being respected, honored, admired, and served. People also want the perceived fame and wealth that comes with leadership. I can understand why this narrative exists; after all, what do you think of when you hear the title, 'CEO'? You think, private jet, you think of someone sitting at the head of the table in a large boardroom, calling the shots. You think about the largest office with glass windows on the topmost floor; you think about million-dollar bonuses and a stock portfolio in the billions. In government, when you think about the head of an agency or a senior executive, what comes to mind? Being part of influential meetings, controlling large budgets, deciding policy, championing initiatives that affect millions of people. These activities whiff of power and influence. However, leadership doesn't always start from there. Sometimes, and for some people like Elsa, it starts with self-doubt, missteps, low confidence, and failure.

I have worked with leaders within the US federal government, academia, and industry for twenty years, and for the last twelve years, I've been the managing director of a small business myself; I have had a front row seat to the rise of leaders who are regular people, doing the hard work of harnessing their ideas and competencies to galvanize people toward accomplishing a goal.

These regular people who become leaders include stories of a single mom who got tired of waiting for her dreams to materialize and started a candle-making company with her personal savings; she grew her company to fifteen employees and $350,000 in annual sales, the first in her family to ever start a business.

A Hispanic American first-generation immigrant who entered public service through the presidential fellows' program and after some years of service is now a branch chief at his agency, leading three major programs and a team of sixty people.

A regular person who became a leader as a young adult, born and raised in a small town in the Midwest US, she took a chance to quit college and market a software product she developed that exploded in the marketplace, and she's suddenly the CEO and founder of a large tech company.

The narrative of leadership that is currently perpetuated in the media, movies, and *Forbes* does not include stories and perspectives of regular leaders like the ones I mentioned who end up doing great things: everyday people who were just good at their job and got promoted to leadership roles, immigrants whose ambition and hard work drove them to build a multimillion-dollar company, tech nerds who are now responsible for stewarding billions of dollars of shareholders' money. I am writing this book to highlight the experiences of these "first ones" and provide a guide for future first ones so they don't feel isolated and can cope with the pressures of leadership.

Leadership on its own is challenging; as a mother, it is a herculean task for me to get four children to agree on what's for dinner without pulling out my "I'm your mother so you'll eat what I give you" card. You'd admit that it can be difficult to get a group of very smart, different people to work together on an initiative. There is a popular saying that "Uneasy lies the head that wears the crown." I submit to you it is twice as challenging when you must lead but have not been taught what to do and how to do it.

Learning by trial-and-error is costly and sometimes painful, especially when you have no precedent for what you are doing, which is the case for the first ones. Even when you have mentors, they are not you. They do not have your unique personality challenges and limitations; they do not have your specific family history, belief systems, and trauma that all mix together to shape your outlook and character as a leader. You can read books or listen to podcasts all day and still feel there is this missing element when it comes to leading for you. As the first one, it is not uncommon to feel like no one understands your journey, that you don't get the support in a way that makes meaning to you. Also, sometimes, you can't even articulate how people can help you because you don't fully know what you need.

If you feel this way, I submit to you it is because you are the first one; no one has ever done what you are trying to do, how you are trying to do it. There is no precedent from your immediate environment that can show you the step-by-step instructions to follow on this journey of leadership. If you feel that no one fully understands your perspective, you are correct because for some of us who are immigrants, outliers, or misfits, it was never in the cards for us to lead. We can thrive when we're just participating, but when it comes to taking the responsibility of leadership, we struggle. We struggle especially with identifying the right mentors and role models because they may have similar work experience as you, but they're not from the same cultural background so they don't understand the institutional, invisible barriers you must overcome to lead. If they are kin to you, they cannot see what you see that is beyond what anyone from the neighborhood or family has accomplished so they cannot relate to you. This is why most first ones feel isolated.

A study conducted by Ron Longwell-Grice, an educator and researcher from the University of Wisconsin, and his colleagues on first-generation college students uncovered that the first ones to attend college face unique challenges across race, gender, and type of school. The researchers studied graduate students at a four-year public university, undergraduates at small private colleges, and Latinos at a two-year institution. They conducted in-depth ninety-minute individual interviews with study participants. They found the students struggled to bring their graduate school and educational experience/identity to their home. One student described this loss as "eclipsing" his family members. Like most graduate students, the participants shared a passion for learning and great enthusiasm for their subjects. They enjoyed discussing big ideas and theoretical concepts.

Ironically, they found the articulation about issues they loved often resulted in an unwanted distance from the family members who had originally encouraged them to attend college. Among the students in four-year and two-year institution, results showed these first-generation students experienced cultural dislocation, a feeling of being lost. Additionally, the study revealed the first ones did not get the amount of financial aid they needed because their parents did not know what other expenses would need to be covered outside tuition. The experience of first-generation students can be likened to first-time leaders. The identity dislocation, the internal battle between what you've seen done before you and what you aspire to be, and the shortage of support, resources, and mentorship, present unique challenges as the first one.

So, what do you do when you're the first one? How do you start to lead when you've never seen anyone lead effectively up close? What do you do when your blind spots as leader start to affect your business, and it seems like your dream is about to die? How do you recover from a crisis due to ignorance that has the potential to end your career? This book provides some context to your experience as the first one and includes tips to successfully blaze the trail. Starting from you, the engine that powers your leadership journey, your people, the vehicle by which your leadership journey travels, and your organization, the system that produces the destination.

The main goal of this book is to validate the leadership experience of the firsts because often, when you are the first one like you to lead in a particular environment, there is an unseen struggle with your leadership journey, and this book highlights that struggle. The main reason is because you have never done what you are trying to do, there may not even be a name for your vision yet, but more challengingly, no one like you has done what you're trying to do, how you plan to do it, in your select environment. Simply put, there is no evidence of successful past performance. There is no historical data that predicts the outcome you're aiming for. This is frightening and confusing. So first, I want to acknowledge all the firsts. You are brave, a change agent, and a trailblazer. I validate your leadership journey.

The second goal of this book is to compile tips you wish you knew and insights to leadership. Firsts don't usually plan to lead, are rarely prepared for it, and often make unforced errors in their leadership journey because no one taught them what to do. If you didn't attend a fancy business school or have parents or family members who were CEOs, politicians, or leaders in academia, how would you know? They certainly don't teach leadership tenets on Twitter, Instagram, or TikTok. I hope you see examples of your experiences as a first in this book and gain new insights on competencies you can build or strengthen in your leadership journey.

If you feel like you never fit in, your vision is so out of the mainframe, you were thrust into a leadership role without preparation, and the lack of preparation has made you lose ground, this book is for you. If you have faced a lot of rejection or are constantly underestimated, ignored, mocked, or criticized for giving voice to your vision because you do not fit the prototype of people who have successfully executed such a vision, this book is for you. If people come to you only when they have problems, take your ideas, and win with them without giving you the credit or platform because you don't yet know how to wield your power, this book is for you. This book is for the outliers, the rejects, the misunderstood, the rarely selected, the underestimated, the others, the first ones.

If this describes you, it is because you are unique; your leadership experience has been frightening and challenging because you are the first one. You belong to an exclusive club of trailblazers, game-changers, disruptors, and fire-starters. If you are the first one in your family to go to college, start a business, earn a PhD, or overcome addiction, or if you are the first black man to hold that position, first Asian female executive of a Fortune 500 company, the first woman politician in your district, the first child to break the poverty cycle in your family, the first Fortune 500 entrepreneur in your community, the first person from your city to win an athletic championship, whatever kind of first you are, I want to invite you on this journey to understand what that position means: why you are the first one, how your life experiences prepared you for your destiny, how to make sense of your call to leadership, how to be comfortable in your uniqueness, and how to gain clarity on who you are called to serve.

This book will help you regardless of the stage you are at in your leadership journey, whether you are new to the awareness of your call to leadership, you've been leading for a while, you're in transition, you're in the middle of a crisis, or you are in your glory years and pouring into the next generation, if you are the first one, this book is for you. How do I know this? I am you.

I am the first of five children, the first in my immediate family to migrate to the US from Nigeria, West Africa, and the first in my family to start a multimillion-dollar government contracting business while nurturing a family and parenting four children. I am a female, immigrant, entrepreneur, executive coach, and mother of four. If I could describe what my experience of leadership has been, I would say I am often underestimated, overlooked, and misunderstood. No one is really expecting me to succeed to the point of bringing my vision fully to life. If I shared details of the full picture of my vision, it would be beyond the comprehension of most people because I can't even wrap my brain around it. I have a vision of developing magnificent leaders of African descent through targeted programs across the continent of Africa and in the diaspora; to some, it does not make sense. What would give me the audacity to think I can do that? Who do I know personally that has executed such a vision on that scale? Nobody. What large organization have I led? None. These are the questions the representatives of the status quo, who reside in my mind, ask me every day I set out to accomplish my vison.

I have successfully run my consulting business for over a decade, leading a team of subject matter experts and senior consultants in the field of technology, business, and government programs. I am also an executive coach certified by the International Coaches Federation (ICF). I work with emerging leaders in government and business to help them build the competencies for magnificent leadership. I help leaders define their own leadership philosophy; identify and influence their target followers; and build a system to continuously fill their mental, physical, and spiritual energy and create shifts in their immediate environments and the world. I work with leaders who are authentic, committed to a lifetime of learning, and skilled at developing people for leadership; they possess the leadership competencies required for success in their field.

I'm bringing my perspective from being a first in many respects, my almost fifteen-year journey in entrepreneurship and lifetime journey of leadership, and my knowledge from formal education and the study of history and the stories of the leaders I work with, coach, and admire. I wrote this book because my path was so unique, the diversity of the hats I wear caused complexities in my journey that were not represented in any story I read on leadership. I've had informal mentors, support, and motivation from biographies, but I had to create my own blueprint for how to be a minister, wife, mother, leader, entrepreneur, immigrant, woman, friend, business owner, employer, and manager, while keeping a sane mind.

There was no blueprint for me because I am the first one. I decided to document what I know now, my learnings over the years about the three components of leadership: leading yourself, leading other people, and leading an organization. In this book, we will discuss what each component of leadership means.

As we walk through the pages together, I invite you, the first one, to gain clarity on your identity and define your unique leadership philosophy, explore your vision, determine what you want to accomplish as a leader, and write it down. I am inviting you to name the skills, abilities, and experiences that thrust you into leadership, and I encourage you to identify the interference stopping you from navigating these challenges and leading effectively. In other words, I want you to take action with the insights you gain from the book. I want you to act on the insights so you can continue to do great things and inspire others to do so too. I have organized magnificent leadership competencies in these three components: Leading yourself, leading people, and leading in an organization. Competencies are the skills, abilities, and knowledge you have. Throughout the book, I mention these competencies, describe their application, and show how to build them and what happens when you are underdeveloped in any one of them.

LEADING YOURSELF

- **self-confidence:** trust in your abilities and experience and believe in your value
- **autonomy:** ability to act on your values and interests, self-govern
- **agency:** capacity to have power, make your own decisions and be responsible for the consequences
- **empathy:** understanding the perspectives and fears of others
- **leadership presence:** a commanding aura with gravitational pull to your ideas, words, and actions
- **decision-making:** ability to identify possible choices, assess implications of each choice, and select one
- **agility:** ability to think and understand complex issues quickly

- **self-awareness:** knowledge of your beliefs and behaviors and how you relate to the world
- **self-management:** ability to manage work and life priorities, responsibilities, and limitations
- **self-regulation:** regulation of emotional triggers
- **resilience:** ability to recover from crisis and stay on mission
- **compassion:** care and concern of others, organizational goals, and mission
- **curiosity and openness:** state of questioning and willingness to learn
- **adaptability:** acceptance of unexpected events and others' ideas
- **initiative:** doing what needs to be done without being asked to
- **digital dexterity:** desire and ability to embrace emerging technology
- **career planning:** taking ownership of your career progression
- **alignment:** synergy with team and organizational culture and goals
- **self-care:** awareness and fulfillment of emotional, physical, spiritual, and relational needs
- **mindfulness:** connection to present moment; to be intentional

LEADING OTHER PEOPLE

- **authenticity:** being who you say you are
- **advocacy:** ability to garner support for a position
- **flexibility:** willingness to let go of strong positions and compromise
- **influence:** persuading others to follow your vision for their benefit
- **delegation:** assigning tasks and scaling productivity
- **achievement drive:** defining excellence and driving it
- **team leadership:** team forming, nurturing, and collaboration
- **effective communication:** active listening, oral and written transmission of messages
- **leading change:** successfully increasing team's adoption of change
- **problem solving**: identifying and managing risk
- **conflict management:** stopping conflict from stalling mission accomplishment

- **consensus building:** getting people on opposing sides of an issue to come to an agreement
- **relationship building:** investing in cultivating and maintaining good relationships
- **establishing trust:** developing rapport and connection with people for dependability
- **organization:** energy, time, and resource management
- **situational awareness:** ability to correctly decode information and data from team members' behaviors and activities
- **inclusivity:** intentionally seeking to understand and valuing people with diverse beliefs, cultures, backgrounds, and experience
- **coaching and people development:** driving growth and behavior change of team members
- **tech savviness:** knowledge of technological trends in your field
- **accountability:** establishing a system of ensuring benchmarks are met
- **championing:** giving credit and praise to team, increasing motivation and inspiration
- **sharing feedback:** reporting back critical information to team members
- **collaboration:** leveraging strengths of a team to create something new
- **civility:** creating a safe working environment by demonstrating respect for all

LEADING AN ORGANIZATION

- **political awareness:** understanding power lines in your organization and with stakeholders
- **domain expertise:** mastery of your organization's business model or industry
- **vision:** seeing what's possible when it's not yet evident
- **strategic thinking:** articulating organizational vision, mission, goals and objectives, and performance indicators
- **brand management:** maintaining organizational presence and reputation

- **crisis management:** sound judgment, quick action, and provision of safety net during a crisis
- **resource management:** best value application of financial and human resources
- **creativity and innovation:** risking failure by trying new things
- **polarity management:** managing unsolvable problems
- **establishing and nurturing culture:** shaping organizational dynamics, structure, and work environment
- **systems thinking:** ability to identify and make sense of patterns, relationships, and contexts
- **budgeting and finance astuteness:** securing funding, managing cash flow and expenses, securing investments
- **strategic alliances:** forging alliance, partnerships, and collaborations for mission accomplishment
- **compliance:** knowledge of and adherence to industry/business regulations, policies, guidelines, and ethics

PART I

LEADING YOURSELF

1

IDENTITY: WHO ARE YOU?

In the movie, *Kung Fu Panda,* Po, the lazy, clumsy, overweight panda, unexpectedly gets chosen to become the Dragon Warrior, a kung fu master, to save the valley from the evil Tai Lung, the greatest threat to their existence. The movie shows the journey of Po coming into the awareness of who he has always been. When he was selected as the Dragon Warrior, the five protectors of the valley were furious and found it comical because, on the outside, he didn't have the looks of the Dragon Warrior. He was not athletic or charismatic, and he didn't fight; why would he? He was the son of a noodle seller. He helped his father, Mr. Ping, a goose, sell noodles in the local market. At least, this is who he was taught he was. One of the most touching yet hilarious scenes of the movie is when Po finds out he was adopted by his father. It is hilarious because Po's friends are surprised he didn't know he was adopted. It seems obvious; biologically, a goose is very different from a panda bear in size, behavior, habits, and so on, but could it be possible that Po saw himself as the father who raised him?

As human beings, we become what we believe. Throughout life, our environment shapes us, teaches us, and sometimes limits us, and we adopt the collective impact of our familial, social, and cultural influences on us as our identity. The dictionary defines *identity* as who or what a person is.

In Po's case, the fact is, he was a giant panda who was raised by a loving father, who happened to be a goose. Po was not a goose. In this chapter, you need to discover the fact of your being. The real you. The original you. Your default settings.

I grew up in Nigeria, West Africa, and was born in a small town called Warri in the south-south region of the country. I am one of the five children of Chief Dr. William Oku Ekeruche. In Warri, everyone knows everyone. Growing up, in a small town, it was not uncommon for people to describe one another by who they were married to or where they worked, or even by an unfortunate circumstance that had befallen them. Yes, Warri was a brutal town to live in if you had an unpleasant life event, because everyone would talk about it, and that event would become the marker by which people identified you and your family. My dad was a medical doctor, and my mom was a dental hygienist. My mom always introduces herself as Mrs. Ekeruche with so much emphasis and pride. You see, my father is from a somewhat prominent family in the south-south region of Nigeria. My uncles and aunties held offices such as chief justice (attorney general) of the state, commissioner (a cabinet post in state government), and local political party leader. My dad was a retired physician. He owned two successful private practices in Warri and in the city of our origin, Obiaruku. So, the name Ekeruche carried weight in my mother's eyes. It denoted honor, prestige, and class. People will often call her "Dr. Wife."

In my culture, this is a huge deal; being a doctor's wife meant you were treated with respect. People assumed you were affluent, and you had influence in society. Nigerian people respect doctors a lot. This was her identity, so it is no wonder that when the ethnic crisis in Warri caused my dad's private practice to crumble, and we had to move out of our fancy home to a small apartment in the office building above my dad's practice, she was devastated (and still is). My siblings and I poke fun at her today about her efforts to bring back the glory days. She still makes it a point to introduce herself as Mrs. Ekeruche. She is constantly measuring people's assessment of her based on whether they remember who she is. Like my mom, it is not uncommon to see women of African descent define themselves by their husbands' status in society, class, or education. The fact is identity cannot be transferred. Even identical twins have different identities, and no matter how much your spouse, sibling, or friends love you, you cannot possess their identity.

Your identity is not the role you play, what position you occupy, or what you own. It is in the intricate and specific weaving together of your spirit, soul, and body. Your identity comes from within, not from the outside; your identity can only be traced to your origin. From a faith perspective, your identity can only be defined by who you believe your creator is; from a science perspective, your identity is the expression of your DNA; and from a psychological perspective, your identity is the unique interweaving of the neurons in your brain that shape the way you think, feel, and choose. Your identity should not change. Identity is innate, definite, and conclusive. It does not depend on your performance or other people's opinions. If you define yourself by your job title, spouse, financial status, fame, or role you play, you are susceptible to an identity crisis because all these things can change.

Knowing your identity is crucial for magnificent leadership because you, the person, are the instrument through which your genius moves into a leadership role. Your identity is part of that light. You must understand what makes you, you. You must have clarity on your innate spiritual, biological, and psychological makeup because this is what grounds you. Once you are clear on who you are, you must accept yourself. All of you. Today, we see an abundance of writings on self-love, but I'd like to take it further and settle on self-acceptance. Self-acceptance is agreeing with your innate biological, spiritual, and psychological makeup. This can be challenging because, let's be honest, there are parts of our biological makeup that are not good, such as a family history of diseases. Also, there are parts of our innate personalities that trip us up in certain scenarios; for example, if your personality type tends to be reserved, it may present a challenge in nurturing relationships. So we tend to want to ignore or discard certain part of ourselves we consider defective instead of humbly accepting our imperfections as the reality of our humanity.

Also, throughout our entire lives, from the educational systems that form us to the images we see in the media, we are constantly being conditioned to believe a narrative about ourselves that is considered optimal but may be different from who we are. All this makes us avoid doing the deep work of gaining clarity on our identity and agreeing with who we are. I always say you don't have to like all aspects of your genetics and personality, but you must accept and agree with yourself as you are.

It is only after you accept your identity and agree with it that you can then master how you apportion yourself in your leadership role. You see, you can apportion yourself in diverse situations when you know your tools. Your spiritual, genetic, and psychological makeup are the tools you have been handed to live with on earth. They are the parts that make the instrument of you. Some of these parts are fast, slow, sharp, blunt, big, or small. They are all important and serve a purpose. When you understand this and know that you oversee how you use the instrument (you), you can pull out a specific part for a particular role, job, or function. This is a core competency of leadership. This helps you demonstrate the competencies of confidence, self-awareness, self-management, and self-regulation.

I would also like to introduce the concept of transformation here. As human beings, the way we express ourselves in the world can change. Our behaviors can change, and what we believe can change, but our DNA, spiritual origin, and personality cannot change. The role of transformation is to adapt and evolve in how we see the parts of who we are and how we apportion those parts; we must avoid trying to change the part itself because we simply cannot do that. If you master this, you will never want to be like anyone else ever again because it is virtually impossible, and you will have a deep level of peace within yourself.

So, what is our spiritual, biological, and psychological makeup? We will dive deeper into these concepts now. Let's start with the spiritual makeup.

Most people will agree that each human being has a spirit, soul, and body. Thomas Merton, the Catholic monk and renowned writer, said, "If a man is to live, he must be alive, body, soul and spirit." *Merriam-Webster* defines *spirit* as an animating or vital principle held to give life to a physical organism. I say it is the nonphysical origination of your life. Other definitions from the dictionary include "the incorporeal part of humans" and "the divine influence as an agency working in the human heart." These definitions show your spirit is what makes you alive. It is the intangible fuel for your living existence.

We don't talk enough about the spirit because it may seem spooky or too arbitrary; it is not the part we can access with our natural senses, but your spirit is real. Also, people shy away from conversations about the spirit because they can be misconstrued for religion. While different religions hold doctrine and dogmas about the spirit being and spirit world, the focus on your spiritual makeup is defining where your spirit originates. When you answer for yourself, who or what gave you life? You are answering the question of what being, beyond your biological parents, is responsible for your existence. Gaining clarity on your spiritual makeup is a nuanced journey. The way to gain clarity may differ based on your religious or cultural beliefs.

There is no right, wrong, good, or bad way to come to know your spiritual makeup, but you must settle on where your life originated. The important thing is to know, accept, and agree with an unseen, beyond-natural origin of your spirit. For example, I was brought up a Catholic; I started catechism at six years old and was raised in the doctrine of the church. During my teenage years, I started to question some of the doctrines and became curious about the topic of human origination. As a science student in college, I took biology courses on evolution. This quest to know the source of my life led me along many paths, and in 2004, at the age of twenty-two, I settled for this understanding of my spiritual makeup: God made me in his image and likeness. Everything about my spiritual makeup is identical to His. I believe God is supreme, without flaw, and cannot change, and my spirit came from Him. God gave me life, and I am His. Every aspect of my spirit is addressed in God's Word, the Bible, so I am never conflicted about my spirit.

This understanding and acceptance of my spiritual makeup serves me well in my leadership journey when I suffer failures and setbacks that lack a natural solution. Whenever I encounter a situation I can't think through, one that is beyond my natural resources, I tap into my spiritual makeup to overcome it and gain victory. Mastering my spiritual makeup also helps me put into perspective my highs, successes, and achievements. I understand there is a higher power that pushes and enables me; after all, there are people who put in more effort in the same environment that didn't get the successful results I got. So, this keeps me level-headed, grounded, and sane. I hope I've been able to illustrate how understanding your spiritual makeup helps you execute as a leader, especially when you are the first to lead. Leadership is tough. Uneasy lies the head that wears the crown. Leadership exposes you to challenges that defy human ability and intellect. Also, leadership opens you up to admiration from people, and fame can drive you over the edge, literally. Your spiritual makeup is your anchor, your stabilizer, and your life-giver.

The soul, which is where the mind is, is also unique for each of us. For the purposes of our discussion, I describe this as your psychological makeup. When discussing identity and psychological makeup, we are not discussing self-image or your inner story about your self-image. Self-image and inner story about self can be affected by external factors such as cultural conditioning and trauma. Here, we are addressing a person's innate psychological intricacies. Specifically, your mental processing: how you think, feel, and choose, how your brain is wired and works, how you take in information and make sense of it, how you interact with the external world, how you feel. To lead from a place of authenticity and manage things well, you must understand your personality type and your behavior patterns.

Research abounds on personality type; there are several personality type assessments you can take to figure out what your personality makeup is. Generally, when it comes to personality and behavior, these assessments score you on attributes like introversion, openness, agreeability, conscientiousness, reliability, and extraversion. These personality type assessments stem from psychological theories that have sought to define the qualitative and quantitative differences between human beings. The earliest personality type indicator theory was Galen's system of four temperaments (Sanguine: Cheerfully optimistic or positive, Choleric: ambitious and fiery, Melancholic: sad and reserved, and Phlegmatic: unemotional and calm), based on the four humors of Hippocrates.

There's also the theory of Type A and Type B personality. According to this theory, Type A individuals are more achievement oriented, and Type B folks are more relaxed. One of the most influential ideas about personality types originated in the work of Carl Jung. Assessments like the Myers-Briggs Type Indicator (MBTI) and Keirsey Temperament Sorter have their roots in Jungian theory. In getting to understand your personality and behavior, it is important to shelve judgment; the tendency to attach good or bad to a personality type prevents us from accepting the full essence of ourselves. These theories should be used to understand differences and distinctions between us as humans and how they show up in our behavior.

The Center for Creative Leadership and Davidson College conducted a study of first-time managers and found the top three challenges they faced are adjustment to people management/displaying authority, developing managerial and personal effectiveness, and leading team achievement. These three most common challenges point to underdevelopment in competency areas like effective communication, leadership presence, time management, influencing, and delegating. These competencies are driven primarily by personality types, behavior, and habits.

The psychological domain of identity carries our mindsets, habits, and frames of reference (how we interpret the stimuli we receive from the world). If our spiritual makeup is the stabilizer and foundation, the psychological makeup is the executor. Understanding your unique personality and mindset is critical in developing the skills of decision-making, emotional regulation, self-management, leadership presence, self-awareness, and situational awareness. These competencies are the medium by which you lead and influence people to work with you to accomplish a goal. These skills help you manage crises, master emotional roller coasters, and come to conclusions on serious matters. Your psychological make-up is very critical to your effectiveness as a leader. Grand View Research reports that the global personal development market size was valued at $41.8 billion and is projected to grow 5.5 percent over the next ten years, primarily due to the growing emphasis on the part of employers on soft skills such as communication and decision-making. This skill enhancement focus of employers for employees is even more important for leaders in organizations. Research over the last twenty years consistently shows the most important leadership qualities are centered around soft skills and emotional intelligence. *Harvard Business Review* conducted a survey of 195 leaders from more than thirty global organizations, and five major themes around leadership effectiveness emerged:

1. High ethical standards and providing a safe environment
2. Empowering individuals to self-organize
3. Promoting connection and belonging among employees
4. Open to new ideas and experimentation
5. Committed to the professional and intellectual growth of employees

According to the research, these themes help magnificent leaders create a safe and trusting environment for the people they lead. This attribute is all about behavior and character. It's about acting consistently with a value system that promotes excellence. I know you're thinking, *I've been with myself all my life, so I think I know my character, and it's pretty good.* Well, it is good that you have this perception of your behavior, but do the people you lead think the same thing? Do you know how they experience you? Are you struggling with a negative behavior pattern? Are there limiting beliefs you hold that are stopping you from growing as a great leader? Getting clarity in your physiological makeup will provide insights to these questions.

Everything I have described earlier on about your psychological makeup is your default setting. It is important to note that from the time we are born, we go through a conditioning process that shapes us to fit cultural norms. Additionally, we experience traumatic events that can affect our mindset and behaviors, and make us develop pseudo identities. For example, research on first-generation immigrants show how vacillating between home culture and culture of the new county can cause misalignment in cultural identity. While in this book, we do not address these components of our psychological makeup that can affect our identity, it is important to note them and observe how we have defined and labelled them as our default setting when it comes to our psychological makeup.

Our bodies hold all our facilities. So, part of our identity is our physical abilities and limitations. If the spirit is the stabilizer and the soul is the executor, the body is the instrument. Our physical bodies and abilities and limitations are part of our identities. Being clear on your identity provides a deep grounding as a leader; leaders who are clear on their identity are always secure and calm, not tossed to and fro by the latest business trends or chaos. Secure and grounded leaders do not compare themselves with others because they accept themselves and the space they occupy.

Leadership is the art and science of using social influence to move people toward a specific goal for their sake. You cannot influence others if you do not know and accept yourself. You can't get people to move toward a long-term goal based on your fame, position, and role alone; when those things change, which they will, your people will stop moving and will no longer be your people. For you to influence people, they need to connect to the real you. They need to see themselves in your vision and your goal.

Getting clear on identity is tough, because from early childhood, culture, society, parental expectations, and institutions feed us information about who we should be. By the time we get to young adulthood, we are layered with people's opinions, societal expectations, cultural expectations, and religious expectations as our identity. Also, by young adulthood, we become soaked in some form of trauma, depending on family history and situation; whether psychological, physical, or sexual trauma, we are ensnared in the vicarious trauma of those around us, our parents' struggles and disappointments, illnesses, family dysfunctions, major life events. These things leave impressions on us that shape how we define our identity, good or bad. Jean Piaget, one of the founding fathers of psychology, said in the preoperational stage, from ages two to seven, a child's brain begins to form and use mental images, symbols, and language. This means that as early as two years old, what you hear, see, and experience is seared into your brain, and you use it to make sense of your world (what happened to you).

I was the first child, and my parents always told me, "You are the first; what you do, the rest will follow." Early on, I developed a pseudo identity around responsibility. My identity became that I am the one who will always do what is right because the others are watching me. While this pseudo identity served me well in some respects and made me disciplined with very little supervision, it led me to automatically take responsibility for people and things that were not mine. When I was eighteen, I moved to the US to attend college, without my parents or siblings; it was a major life event, and another identity crisis started. Now I was the responsible one, who will always do what is right, in a foreign land with pretty much no guidance. I had to quickly learn the American culture, the school system, working system, and paying bills (in Nigeria, I never heard of bills). I had to learn American English, which is quite different from British English I grew up with. To adapt to the new society, I took on another pseudo identity, Nigerian American, African American, American Nigerian, working on my accent, mannerisms, to adapt while not losing my rich culture and African heritage. Talk about identity crisis.

Then I entered the workforce, and my role as a worker introduced me to take on another pseudo identity to portray proficiency. In the workplace, we are expected to perform, to demonstrate we are adding value to the organization; that is how we are rated. Even when we face discrimination and challenges, we just keep churning out deliverables and producing. Then I got married, another major life event. I joined my life to another human being's life; within the context of my culture, as a wife, I am expected to absorb my husband's vision of life and align to it. Another major identity crisis; how can two people from different backgrounds, with different personalities, join and live one life? Oh, I know how: assume another pseudo identity, because I am the responsible one, and it is my job to assume the identity required for this part of my life. I assume the responsibility of the loyal partner; that's what being a wife meant to me. I became the "I am rocking with you forever" wife.

Then I have kids; whew … whole human beings came out of me. I am their mother. Based on societal and cultural expectations, mothers are sacrificial lambs. Oh, that's easy; I will assume that pseudo-identity too. Great, so now, I'm a savior. From the age of nineteen, I was an entrepreneur; I sold home security systems door to door, sold Cutco knives door to door, sold accessories while in college, and became a licensed real estate agent. I always had a side business with a full-time job while going to school. After getting married, I entered federal services, but I quit my good, stable government job to pursue a consulting and professional services business to have more time with the family, not realizing that leadership is more time-consuming and demanding than followership. My business, AMA Consulting, has grown to a multimillion-dollar enterprise that provides professional and information technology services to the federal government.

None of my family members or friends started the type of business I started and am currently running, so I had to create everything from scratch: service offering, business infrastructure, team, and so on; that required another pseudo-identity. Now I am a creator. A responsible, Nigerian, African American, performer, loyal partner, sacrificial lamb, creator became my identity, even though it was far from who I was. This led to stress, burnout, confusion, fragmented mindset, angry outbursts, and critical judgments. It took so much energy just to show up as these multiple identities every day in my relationships, business, much less showing up for myself. It made me a narrow thinking leader, always the last person to know about a risk, an unapproachable leader who led from a place of fear, fear of people, fear of failure, fear of success, fear of everything. On the outside, I looked successful, but on the inside, I was dying.

I was still very efficient acting in my pseudo identity. I got my MBA and successfully launched my business; it grew every year in revenue, but internally, I was conflicted and stuck. I was paralyzed by fear, tired, and unhappy. I always knew, though, that I was destined for great things. I always had a desire to develop people in leadership, always wanted to serve the world. I could not move past a certain point. I felt stuck.

In 2019, I got serious about doing the work of self-discovery and healing. I invested in therapy and coaching, and it changed my life. I started to get to the bottom line of my identity, but I am still on the journey of accepting my identity.

You see, knowing your identity is one thing, but accepting yourself for who you are is another thing. Accepting your innate makeup, your physiology, your genetics, your psychological makeup, your place of origin, your family, your own life for what it is, is hard. Most times, we want our identity to be what we created to gain acceptance from society and validation from people. However, it is not sustainable to live in a pseudo reality all your life. To accept your identity, you must lose the need to be accepted by others. When you first start on this journey and begin to accept yourself, you may begin to lose relationships with people who connected with your pseudo identity; despite what people say, very few people are ready to make the investment to really know another person, to know the complexities of their human experience. Therefore, we suffer from imposter syndrome. We fear we will accidentally reveal our true selves, and we will not be accepted. We expend resources trying to stay in our pseudo identities so we can maintain the perfect world and systems we have created. But I have one question, in Dr. Phil's voice: How is that working for you? I have heard people define imposter syndrome as self-doubt, but what is the source of self-doubt? A lack of acceptance of who you are, because if you value you, you will accept you. Acceptance of self is the action that signifies awareness of self-worth.

Why is knowing your identity and accepting your identity important? It is important because to be successful as a leader, you must demonstrate these qualities:

1. **Decisiveness:** the timely ability to use sound judgment to initiate action, to move action forward, and to make an impact
2. **Authenticity:** the ability to express the fact of who you are and what you believe in, so others can relate to you and trust you

3. **Influence:** harnessing the genius of others to achieve a goal so you can accomplish a larger scale of success

4. **Emotional intelligence:** having a good relationship with yourself and others so you build leverage and political capital for use in critical moments and in times of crises

These leadership competencies require identity clarification and acceptance as a foundation. One of the traits of a leader is clarity and acceptance of the fact of their being. Leaders who are clear on their innate compositions (good or bad) are self-aware, relatable, and convincing; they can self-regulate, manage emotions, make decisions when it matters, communicate effectively, and influence others.

For leaders who are just beginning their leadership journey, the first ones, unclear, fragmented, pseudo identity shows up in four main ways:

CONFUSION

Have you ever worked for bosses who change their mind all the time? Leaders who were scared to make decisions, always punting the ball, blaming others, or missing in action during a time of crisis because they didn't know what to do? How did that make you feel? Were you clear on the goals, mission, and what was expected of you? Did you feel like you could rely on them in times of crisis? I bet you were not. I bet you felt like you were always on thin ice because you didn't get a sense of stability and security from them. John Maxwell says a leader is one who "knows the way, goes the way, and shows the way." If you don't lead from the fact of who you are, you will be reactionary in your decision-making, following trends, seeking to be popular, and taking advantage of events. This may serve you temporarily, but over time, people will become confused because of the lack of consistency and stability. This confusion can lead to toxicity and burnout. I worked in an office that changed the process on how to conduct compliance checks for federal programs four times in one year. Program participants were confused, not knowing what they needed to do to maintain compliance; calls and complaints started to come in. The team was frustrated because it took so much time to educate program participants on new processes, and shortly after, it will change again. Our leader was doing her best trying to satisfy all the regulatory requirements and desires of senior leaders, but there was a lot of confusion, and it led to massive turnover. Sometimes, you must sacrifice likeability or agreeability for stability. There is so much chaos in the world, and people are looking for leaders who can provide stability and consistency; they want a leader they can depend on and know what to expect. This is why even when a bad leader is consistent, even on a morally wrong topic, people follow them.

CONTROL

Magnificent leaders use social influence to get people on board with their vision, not command and control. Even in the military or traditional religious organizations where leaders give orders, the people who follow them give consent by voluntarily joining the organization. As a leader, you control things and events, not people. You cannot control another human being without instilling fear. As an executive coach, I see managers doing this all the time, using threats, being passive-aggressive with employees who don't do what they want, being verbally abusive to employees who are struggling, I call it the do-this-or-else approach. What happens when they call your bluff and do it anyways? What do you do then? Even as a parent, you can tell your children what to do in their formative years; once they grow up, they have autonomy.

People will always become free of what you use to control them. A more advantageous way to get people on board is through social influence. Social influence is building rapport with your followers, making them see themselves in you and showing them why what you need them to do is important and of value to them. This requires authenticity; people can see through smoke and mirrors fast. They know when you are showing them a side of you just to get them to do something. They know when you are not one of them but pretend to be. They know when you really do not understand where they're coming from and what they need, but you say you do. Building rapport with people is sometimes admitting you don't know where they're coming from and what is important to them and being humble to learn. If their commitment and engagement is significant to your vision as a leader, then it is worth it to make the investment to build rapport.

When I coach leaders, one of the most common questions they come to me with is, "How do I get people to cooperate with me and do the work?" It starts with rapport from relationship building. From the beginning, as you are building your team, relate authentically, show people your leadership philosophy early, let them know what to expect, be honest, and paint the picture of the job/role as clearly as you can. I heard a consultant describe interviews as two people lying to each other. The employer is trying to convince the applicant the job is rewarding, and the company is the best place to work, and the potential employee is selling her or his credentials. Leading with authenticity is far more difficult than control. It requires vulnerability, humility, and intentionality.

Nelson Mandela had a group of friends and his senior leaders who were in the fight with him for freedom from apartheid in South Africa. The movie, *Mandela,* portrays how Mandela demonstrated this leadership competency of authenticity so well; even though he was their leader, he invested in building and establishing rapport with his team. First, they knew him; they knew the core of his approach was forgiveness. Even though it was hard for some of them to come on board with that, because of the evil that was done to them and their people, they followed his approach. He was always honest with them. When he was called in for negotiations for his release, he always weighed their perspective and the impact of what he agreed to on them; this made them secure that he would always look out for them. At some point, Mandela was offered freedom from jail alone, and he refused to accept the offer if his comrades were not going to be free too. This is why even in the prison, he led not only his comrades but wardens and eventually the head warden, who eventually granted his request to wear long pants. There is something compelling about authenticity, because at the end of the day, as human beings, we all want the same things and struggle with the same core issues in different formats, regardless of what we look like, what we believe, or where we come from. The alternative approach of control can quickly become abusive and counterproductive. Control forces you as a leader to devise more means to gain leverage for control, and this can create desperation and resort to threats and verbal abuse and cause serious damage.

INSECURITY

One of my favorite stories in the Bible is the parable of the prodigal son (Luke 15:11—32). It goes like this: A wealthy king had two sons. One day, the younger of the two went to his father and asked for his inheritance. The father gave it to him, and he squandered it living a lavish lifestyle in a faraway country. He lost all his money and became broke to the point of eating out of a pig's pen. One day, he had an epiphany, or as I like to describe it, he remembered who he was. And he said to himself, "Even my father's servant has a better life than what I'm living now." Can you imagine eating the leftovers of pigs? How degrading, humiliating, pathetic it was to literally feel like you were subordinate to pigs. This young man had to get to this low place to finally gain clarity and accept his identity. He went back to the same father he dishonored and was willing to take a lesser position as a servant in his life instead of son.

What prompted his foolish actions in the first place? Insecurity. Insecurity comes when you believe lies that you have no value, and you don't measure up. When do you start to believe the lie? When you lose sight of your identity and remove focus from the fact of your being and your innate spiritual, psychological, and biological makeup. The truth is, the prodigal son already had what he asked his father for; his inheritance was his at that time and after his father passed on. Inheritances have a timeline and condition attached. But somehow, he started to believe the lie that he would not get it, so to take matters into his hands, he asked for it now. Where did that lie come from? Was it his mind feeding him toxic thoughts? Was it a result of doubt taking hold in his character from previous disappointments? Or maybe he was constantly compared to his older brother (the responsible one), highlighting his limitations. As a magnificent leader, you must be in touch with the fact of who you are, every day, and accept yourself to quell the sting of insecurity.

When you are in front as a leader, people think they have a right to have an opinion about everything about you. The first ones are often criticized, sized up, compared to others, analyzed. One minute, people praise your genius; the next, they castigate you for being human, as if you could be anything else. If you lose your grip on your identity for whatever reason, insecurity eats you for breakfast, lunch, and dinner; you will become consumed by what others think and say about you, to the point of being stoic as a leader. Insecurity will cause you to sabotage those who are committed to your vision coming to reality because of your fear of the negative, self-fulfilling prophesy of uselessness coming to pass. You will become a slave to striving and grinding to prove your worth. Insecurity will send you into the pig's pen to get something you already have.

Insecure leaders cannot give praise or publicly acknowledge the accomplishment of others. They also find it hard to delegate. They always want to be on the stage. They live off the praise of others; they don't trust their instincts and don't believe in their own worth. Insecure leaders are bullies. They live in a prison cell, trying to prevent anyone from seeing their weaknesses. They are always on the edge and in the middle of conflict. They never say what they truly believe because they are calculating where to land on issues to look like the boss. For some leaders, this has become a full-time occupation. They make decisions solely to prove or disprove something. It is a very exhausting way to live and is not sustainable. I know because I used to be a very insecure leader. My insecurity came from being heavily criticized and bullied, so I started a crusade to prove them wrong, getting into anything and everything to achieve the world's definition of success. First of all, there is no "them"; them is a self-preserving mental construct to keep us paranoid. Fear is a self-preserving mechanism.

While I was in college and in grad school, I always had a full-time job and ran two businesses. As quickly as I amassed this so-called success, it was gone. I got a house in 2005 to prove I was not useless but successful, using a loan from a predatory lender; the following year, the mortgage ballooned, and I couldn't keep up. I filed chapter 13 bankruptcy to stop the foreclosure and still lost the house in 2007, newly married with a baby. It was horrible. I have been to the pigpen, and it is not a nice environment. It stinks so bad, and everyone can smell it on you, even after you leave there. One of the reasons I wrote this book is to help you avoid the pigpen. The first ones struggle with serious insecurities because they lose touch with their identity on the way to being first. Just know that when people compare you to others, mock you, or criticize you, it is not your job to prove them wrong. A strong identity helps you not succumb to that pressure to prove people wrong and stay the course of your own journey.

There is one more way identity distortion affects you: underperformance.

UNDERPERFORMANCE

As a human being, you never know what you are capable of if you don't know who you are. In the Disney movies discussed earlier, Po would never have been able to defeat the villain if he didn't first realize he was the Kung Fu Panda, and Elsa would not have been able to save her country if she didn't realize she had magical abilities. A lot of people are living and performing beneath their capacity because they do not know who they are. Your unique superpower lies in your identity. It is not out there; it is in you. Your spiritual, psychological, and physical being carries immense power to change nations, introduce new trends, create new solutions to solve the budding problems in the world.

Without understanding your power and how to use it, you may not know your place in the world. You may be in the early stages of self-discovery and are still not sure about what your role is in your community and the world. You may have self-doubt and question if you have anything meaningful to offer the world. This is what people call purpose. Your purpose is uncovered in your identity. People often think that purpose is achieved by doing. It is not; it is achieved by being your true self. When you are who you truly are (identity), you unlock the recessive powers inside you to do what you were created to do (purpose). This is what brings optimum performance and success as I define it. Performance refers to the level of effectiveness and efficiency with which an individual, team, or organization carries out specific tasks, duties, or activities to achieve desired outcomes or goals. It is a measure of how well objectives are accomplished and how efficiently resources (such as time, effort, and money) are utilized in the process.

Having identity clarification and acceptance is the foundation of your leadership philosophy. Identity is in the spiritual, psychological, and physical domain. Your identity cannot change, but you use it in different roles and seasons of life which continue to evolve as you grow and expand fully into the utmost expression of yourself. Strong identity knowledge and acceptance helps make you an authentic, decisive, emotionally intelligent, influential leader. As an emerging leader, the first one, having pseudo identity, fragmented identity, and lack of self-acceptance can make you controlling and insecure when you lead and create an environment of confusion. As you begin the journey of accepting your true identity and investigating it, I offer you these tips that have helped me and helped the leaders I coach:

1. **Practice Self-Compassion:** Be kind and gentle with yourself, just as you would be with a close friend. Acknowledge your imperfections and treat yourself with the same compassion and understanding you extend to others.

2. **Challenge Negative Self-Talk:** Become aware of negative thoughts and self-criticisms. Challenge them by questioning their validity and replacing them with positive and affirming statements about yourself.

3. **Focus on Your Strengths:** Recognize and celebrate your strengths and accomplishments. Shift your focus from perceived weaknesses to your positive attributes and the unique qualities that make you who you are.

4. **Embrace Your Imperfections:** Understand that being human means having flaws and imperfections. Embrace them as a natural part of life and an essential aspect of your individuality.

5. **Set Realistic Expectations:** Set achievable goals for yourself per time. Realize that you don't have to do everything at once. Pace yourself according to your own life journey and avoid comparing yourself to others, and instead focus on your own progress and growth.

6. **Forgive Yourself:** Let go of past mistakes and forgive yourself for any perceived failures or regrets. Understand that making mistakes is a part of learning and growing as a person.

7. **Surround Yourself with Supportive People:** Surround yourself with positive and supportive individuals who appreciate and accept you for who you are. Avoid toxic relationships that undermine your self-acceptance and force you to create a pseudo identity to be accepted.

8. **Practice Mindfulness:** Engage in mindfulness practices to stay present in the moment, without judgment. This helps cultivate a nonjudgmental awareness of your thoughts and feelings and gives you clarity on your mental processing, thinking patterns, and feelings.

9. **Engage in Self-Care:** Prioritize self-care and engage in activities that bring you joy and fulfillment. Taking care of your physical, emotional, and mental well-being fosters self-acceptance.

10. **Seek Professional Support:** If you struggle with self-acceptance, consider seeking guidance from a therapist or counselor who can help you navigate your feelings and develop a healthy sense of self.

11. **Remind Yourself of Your Worth:** Create positive affirmations and reminders of your worth and repeat them daily. Reinforcing positive beliefs about yourself can gradually foster self-acceptance.
12. **Learn from Mistakes:** Instead of dwelling on mistakes, view them as opportunities for growth and learning. Embrace a growth mindset that welcomes challenges and sees failures as stepping stones toward improvement.

Remember that self-acceptance is a journey, and it's okay to have ups and downs along the way. Be patient with yourself and commit to the process of embracing and accepting your identity. Here are some tips to discover your innate identity and break out of your pseudo identity:

1. **Journaling:** Keep a journal to jot down your thoughts, feelings, and experiences. Writing can help you gain insights into your psychological makeup.
2. **Seek Solitude:** Spend time alone in quiet reflection. Solitude provides an opportunity to connect with your inner thoughts and feelings, without external distractions.
3. **Notice Patterns and Recurring Themes:** Pay attention to patterns that emerge in your life and family; they will give you insight into your natural proclivities.
4. **Seek Feedback from Others:** Ask for feedback from friends, family, or mentors about your strengths and unique qualities, and the impact you have on others. External perspectives can complement your self-discovery journey.
5. **Read and Educate Yourself:** Study your history, read books and articles, and take courses related to personal development and self-discovery. Learning about different aspects of yourself can enlighten you about your spiritual and psychological makeup.
6. **Take Assessments:** Psychometric assessments abound that can give you insight into your personality and behavior; examples are DISC, Myers-Briggs, and Clifton Strengths. Also, medical and psychological assessments provide insight into your biological and mental makeup.

2

WHAT IS THE SIZE OF YOUR CUP?

CAPACITY

Once upon a time in a small town, there lived a loving father named John. He was a hardworking man who always believed he could handle anything life threw at him. He had a happy family with his wife, Sarah, and two children, Emily and Michael.

One day, a sudden and unexpected crisis struck their family. Sarah fell seriously ill and had to be hospitalized. The doctors were concerned about her condition, and John felt his world crumbling around him. He had always been the pillar of strength for his family, but this time, he felt powerless.

As the days turned into weeks, John found himself juggling work, taking care of the children, and spending time at the hospital with Sarah. He tried his best to maintain a positive outlook for Emily and Michael, but he couldn't hide his worry and fear.

Despite all his efforts, John realized he couldn't do it all alone. He started neglecting his own well-being, losing sleep, and skipping meals. He was burning out, and it was affecting his ability to be there for his family.

One evening, while sitting by Sarah's bedside, John's eyes filled with tears. He held her hand tightly and admitted, "I don't know if I can handle this. I've always believed I could be strong for us, but I feel overwhelmed."

Sarah smiled weakly and replied, "John, it's okay to feel overwhelmed. We're in this together, and it's alright to ask for help."

With Sarah's encouragement, John reached out to his friends and family for support. They stepped in to take care of the children, bring meals, and provide emotional comfort. John realized he didn't have to carry the weight of the crisis on his shoulders alone.

As Sarah's condition remained critical, John learned to accept his limitations. He couldn't fix everything, and that was okay. He discovered the power of leaning on others for strength and comfort during difficult times.

Through the crisis, John learned the importance of self-care. He began taking breaks to rest and recharge, understanding that he could better support his family when he took care of himself too.

In the midst of the family crisis, John and Sarah's bond deepened. They found solace in each other's love and support, and they appreciated every moment they had together.

As weeks turned into months, Sarah's condition started to improve slowly. The crisis had been a test of their family's resilience, and they emerged stronger and more united than ever before.

John learned that being a father and a husband didn't mean having all the answers or being invincible. It meant being there for his family, being vulnerable, and knowing when to ask for help. He realized that true strength came not from pretending to be infallible, but from embracing his humanity and the love and support of his family and friends.

And so, as life moved forward, John continued to be a loving father, husband, and friend, cherishing every moment with his family and appreciating the beauty of life, even in the face of challenges. The family crisis had taught him the valuable lesson that while he may have limits, the power of love and togetherness could overcome any obstacle that life threw their way.

Collings Dictionary defines *human capacity* as the amount of something you can do. As leaders, we are vessels through which creativity and wisdom are applied to the people we lead and the things we manage. Leadership requires expending mental, psychological, and emotional resources. For example, the leadership competency of problem solving requires use of critical thinking, flexibility, and energy. You may know what these competencies are and how to execute them, but do you know how much of them you have? The concept of capacity may sound foreign here because leaders are visionary, and like John in this story, we often plunge into projects, causes, and business with only the goal in mind; he tried helping his wife recover while caring for the entire family alone, without accounting for the work it would take to meet the goal. Do you as a leader have the capacity to put in that work by yourself?

In today's culture, we hear these motivational phrases: "You can be anything you want to be if you put your mind to it" and "The sky is your limit." While these are great slogans to motivate you, inspire you, and get you going, as a leader, you need to know your abilities firsthand to finish the job.

To illustrate the central point I'm making here, I will discuss capacity as a countable noun. For example, the capacity of a machine is its size in horsepower. The size of the house a generator can power, for example, depends on the horsepower the generator has. Smaller horsepower generators can power smaller units, while a large horsepower generator can power an entire commercial building. Both generators produce the same thing but have different limits.

Conversely, a three-hundred-seat theater will hold fewer people than a sixty-thousand-seat stadium. Both buildings generally have the same purpose but different capacities. While both venues can be used for events, the type of events suitable for the venue will be different. I hope you're beginning to get the picture now.

Thomas Griffiths, a Princeton University psychologist and computer scientist, wrote an article to explain the uniqueness of artificial intelligence by studying human intelligence through human limitations. Griffiths argued that humans have a limited amount of time to learn. Nature may only provide a limited number of opportunities to learn behaviors relevant to survival, and the length of human lives imposes an upper bound or limit on the amount of data available to an individual. For example, computers can be programmed to store 100 times the amount of information in five minutes that a human being can gain by reading in a year.

Second, Griffiths said humans have a single brain with limited processing power and so can only do limited computations. Lastly, he claimed human minds have limited communication. There is no way to directly transfer the contents of one person's brain to another. Recent breakthroughs in artificial intelligence have been driven by an exponential increase in the amount of computation being used to solve problems. It is common to see computer systems that hold the experiences of many lifetimes of humans. Also, the results of these systems can be easily copied to one another.

Magnificent leaders not only know what they are good at but know their limitations when it comes to capacity. Understanding your limits will help you build a team with complimentary qualities and attributes to move your mission forward. Like John, we need to enlist our neighbors, friends, and family to help us reach our goal. Not being acquainted with your limits exposes you to negative consequences, or blind spots.

In leadership, a blind spot is an opening for risk you have not yet identified. Blind spots are the major causes of unforced errors in decision-making, communication, and action. Bono, the famous musician, said, "Every age has its massive moral blind spots. We might not see them, but our children will."

What you don't know can expose you to harm because you don't have the opportunity to prepare for it. Most times, it takes someone else to uncover a blind spot in us, because we often see ourselves the way we want to be seen, not how people experience us. We can also uncover our blind spots through reflecting on a series of negative patterns that show where the opening for risk is in our character or approach. There is an old saying that what you don't know won't kill you. What you don't know may not kill you, but it may cause you to make costly mistakes, slow you down, clog your creativity, and stifle your productivity.

In terms of leadership capacity, the capacity you have can be measured in three major ways: intuition, leadership presence, and character.

INTUITION

Intuition is the ability to understand something instinctively, without reason. It is to access knowledge and apply it properly, quickly, and confidently. Intuition gets stronger through mastery. According to influential research by psychologist Anders Ericsson, the path to mastery is available to anyone who is prepared to put in the necessary amount of practice. His research of elite musicians, athletes, and chess players suggested they practiced at least ten thousand hours, spread over a period of more than ten years. Ericsson said not just any practice will do; it must be deliberate practice on a particular subject. This requires tireless effort, multiple bouts of failure, and a dogged ability to keep dusting yourself up and trying again.

When Bill Gates dropped out of Harvard in 1975 to start Microsoft, his intuition told him he was going to be successful. There was no evidence, but he understood something that was not obvious to the eye. Why? Where did that understanding originate from? Let's learn more about his history to find out. He was born in Seattle, Washington, to William Henry Gates Sr. and Mary Maxwell Gates. His father was a prominent lawyer and his mother served on the board of directors for First Interstate Bank and the United Way. At thirteen, he was enrolled in an exclusive preparatory school. In the eighth grade, the mothers club at the school used the proceeds from a rummage sale to purchase a Teletype Model 33 ASR terminal and a bloc of computer time on a General Electric computer for students.

Gates loved programming and was excused from his math class to pursue his passion for programming. He wrote his first computer program on this machine. By the time Gates was a junior in college, he was already almost at the mastery level when it came to programming. He had over eight years of dedicated practice. So that hunch or instinct (or risk, as it would seem to some people) was founded on a bed of confidence of eight years of practice.

Environmental factors such as privilege, access, and exposure feed one's instinct. After Gates started Microsoft, his mother facilitated his first contract with IBM through her corporate contracts, according to the *New York Times*. Mrs. Gates was a very influential woman in the community. In 1975, she became the first woman to serve as director of First Interstate Bank and was the first woman to serve as president of the King County's United Way. It is no coincidence that it was the same year her son dropped out of Harvard to start his company. Remember the mom's club in Bill's school? Why would they purchase a Teletype Model 33 ASR terminal and block off computer time from GE? That seems like a very odd investment for a high school to make. I am speculating that his very influential mother had picked up on her son's interest in computers and used her influence to start him on the right path by giving him access to practice and helping him secure his first contract.

When it comes to intuition, acting on instinct, there must be something that is the basis of that inner knowing. It is either exceptional talent or mastery. The sharpness of your intuition is related to the level of your talent and mastery. You see leaders who can make moves on the fly; they have mastered that industry and instinctively know what will work and what will not work. When you meet leaders who can bring people from different perspectives to the table and secure a deal, they have mastered the art of negotiation and personalities. I once coached a leader who was a retired chief information officer of a federal agency. She said young CIOs often called on her for advice about organizational challenges they were experiencing, and she would tell them various actions they could take and the outcome for each. Those who didn't take her counsel seriously would often come back to her and ask, "How did you know what going to happen?" She was often called a witch. She is not a witch; she just had very strong intuition because she has mastered the role of CIO within a federal agency. It was because she served in that role for thirty-two years; she learned the administrative, human capital, legal, and political aspects of the role. She learned from challenges and setbacks she experienced in that role; she knew the ins and outs of it. She was a master at it, so her intuition was very strong.

The strength of your instinct is a critical component of your capacity.

As a leader, you cannot be in the weeds and have every detail all the time. Your operational intelligence comes from people, data, and your instincts. To develop your instincts, you need access and opportunity to practice and gain mastery. This capacity issue comes up a lot for the first one. The firsts rarely have the access and opportunity to put in their ten thousand hours to gain mastery. I was fortunate to have guardian angels in managers and colleagues turned mentors, like Jane Pierson, a senior partner at the first consulting firm I worked for, who encouraged me to go for my MBA and told me about the Georgetown Executive Coaching program.

After graduating with my bachelor's in psychology and working for a few years, I was torn between going to law school and getting a master's degree. While working at Jane's consulting firm, I started to show real interest in the behavior assessments they conducted for leaders. I helped them plan the leadership offsites for executive directors and federal leaders. I started reading books on leadership from the bookshelf in the downtown DC office. The first book I read was *Servant Leadership* by Robert K. Greenleaf.

One day, Jane walked to my office and said to me, "Maria, I see you're interested in being a consultant. You are very smart, but no one will allow you to practice on them. You need to get your credentials. You need an MBA."

Jane connected me with her colleague in UMUC, who encouraged me to apply for the MBA program, and I did, and I finished it. That MBA opened doors for me, specifically entry into federal service. After I left federal service and started consulting full time, I had lunch with Jane and shared with her how I didn't feel very confident in my abilities. I struggled a lot with being in front; based on my personality type, I prefer to work in the background. But here I was, had started a consulting practice, and I was not going to fail, but insecurities were hindering me.

Jane said to me, "Maria, you are a gifted consultant and coach. You know how to quickly assess situations, seek out solutions, and form a team to implement them. You also have exceptional speaking skills, but you need to put it all together. I will connect you to a colleague who attended an executive coaching program. This program will help you build your confidence."

I applied to that program two days before the deadline and got in. That program was one of the most significant defining moments of my life and career. I was exposed to teachers who were senior leaders in various organizations and coached the best of the best. I learned the culture of learning and cultivated the habit of reading continuously and acquiring credentials in my career. What seems like the natural knack I have for influencing people, motivating people, teaching, coaching, came from years of mastery. As a leader, you must give yourself the time to strengthen your intuition. This can be hard to quantify because intuition is not something that is readily obvious.

It is often used by leaders behind the scenes in their toughest moments; it is used when leaders are seeking a solution that has defied other interventions. Intuition is used when leaders are looking to unleash what's locked up inside themselves and to get to a new place. The strength of your instinct speaks to your capacity to lead. We have created a society that honors the servant and has forgotten the gift. As a leader, if you rely only on tried and proven policies and prescribed courses of action, your organization will become stagnant and stale. Intuition is that gut feeling that guides you to uncover the unknown. Magnificent leaders do great things; they articulate groundbreaking ideas and turn them into billion-dollar companies. Leaders with low intuition overanalyze and second-guess, always afraid to make a mistake; they miss a big risk or great opportunity. Leaders with high intuition make crisp decisions and evolve.

As a leader, have you ever gotten a sense that something was off with your team, or that a particular partner may not pan out to be who they presented themselves to be, or have you ever gotten a hunch to start an initiative that may not be popular? This is how intuition often shows up in daily work; we often ignore it for the sake of speed and perfection. We are often in a hurry to make decisions, so we just do what we've always done. Sometimes, we ignore our intuition because we are afraid of the outcome of making decisions that are not data driven; how do you go before your board and say you have a gut feeling that this partnership will not get us to our goals? A leader does not do what is always popular; a leader does what is right. You are the master; if your heart is telling you something is not right, investigate it. If you have a gut feeling to make a move, do it. It may be what launches you into a higher level in your career or business. Tapping into your intuition and listening to it gives you originality as a leader.

Your ability to use intuition speaks to your capacity as a leader.

Here are some tips to sharpen your intuition:

1. **Practice solitude:** Because intuition comes from within, the best way to be in touch with it is to spend time alone to conduct an internal scan of your reception to the information you have available to you.
2. **Conduct reviews of your past decisions:** Review your past decisions and actions; what worked and what didn't? Take note of when you've been right about an assessment you made. It will help you trust your intuition more.
3. **Just do it:** Reasoning is the number one blocker of intuition; sometimes, just do it. Don't try to get stuck in a reasoning loop.

LEADERSHIP PRESENCE

Leadership presence is the effect you have on people when they are around you. This is another yardstick that is used to measure capacity for leaders. As a leader, people must respect and trust you. People who have met former President Bill Clinton or Barack Obama explain what it is like to meet them. They describe euphoria when they're in their presence. They feel connected. A former colleague of mine who had met President Clinton during campaign events described his eye contact as magnetic; he said, "When you shake hands with him, in a room of thousands of people, he makes you feel like you are the only person in the room." Some entertainers are paid to just make an appearance at an event because their presence alone will increase attendees for the event or boost sales.

This presence is a combination of confidence, charisma, and excellent oratory skills. Movie stars and entertainers have this magnetic presence that draws people in and holds their attention. Entertainer, Beyoncé Knowles has been called the celebrity of celebrities. She has a very strong leadership presence. When she enters a room, everyone notices. She commands attention effortlessly. When she's performing live, it is almost like a religious experience. Her fans, the beyhive, follow her religiously; when her apparel IVY Park, in her partnership with Adidas, drops, it sells out in minutes. Try criticizing her on social media, and the beyhives will come after you. Her presence is so strong that she can drop a single or album without prior advertising and win Grammys. She holds the record of the most Grammys won by a woman; she has won a staggering twenty-eight of them and twenty-nine MTV video music awards, making her the most decorated artist in the award show history and the most awarded artist in the Soul Train and BET awards too.

Leadership presence plays a huge role in influencing people and motivating them to action. This adds to your capacity. Beyoncé's success is more than talent and effort; presence plays a huge role in the success of her brand. Leadership presence affects your capacity to influence people and motivate them to action. Beyond having talent or subject matter expertise, you need strong leadership presence; you need to be able to speak to people with conviction, clarity, and compassion. You need to demonstrate self-assuredness when you step into the room, and you need a reputation that precedes you before you enter the room.

If you have all the charisma, oratory prowess, and confidence without good character and a great reputation as the foundation, your leadership presence may attract people, but you will not be able to hold their attention and influence them for long because people will always find you out.

The amount, level, and effect of leadership presence you have speaks to your capacity to lead. While leadership presence cannot be qualified numerically, people know if you have it or not, and they respect you, connect to you, and take action based on the strength of your presence. Presence has various components such as character, confidence, charisma, and oratory prowess. Let's dive deeper into these components and explore how they affect your capacity to lead.

CHARACTER

Character refers to the combination of moral and ethical qualities that define an individual's personality, values, beliefs, and behavior. It encompasses a person's integrity, honesty, responsibility, empathy, and other virtuous traits that guide their actions and interactions with others.

Character plays a crucial role in leadership presence, which refers to the impact and influence a leader has on others. As a leader, when you have strong positive character, you are seen as trustworthy. When people trust you as the leader, they are more likely to follow your guidance and direction; this leads to you having increased influence and effectiveness. Character enhances your credibility as a leader, and this is leadership presence. Credibility means that people can vouch for you. This is what people mean when they say your reputation precedes you. When you consistently demonstrate integrity and ethical behavior, your words and actions carry more weight. If you are a perfume collector, then you know the difference between Eau de Parfum and Eau de Toilette, the former has a longer lasting scent than the latter. As a leader, you want to grow into being Eau de Parfum as regards leadership presence.

As a leader, every word that comes out of your mouth must carry weight, execute something, and shift mindsets; your words should be potent and long lasting. This is why magnificent leaders are measured and deliberate in their words. Leaders with strong character are authentic in their interactions; they operate from the universal code of wrong and right. Whenever you see leaders who have their own version of the truth or what is right, they lack character. Leaders with great character remain true to their values and principles, which fosters a genuine and transparent leadership style and an authentic leadership philosophy. Character helps leaders remain resilient in the face of challenges. Leaders with a strong sense of character are better equipped to handle setbacks, maintain composure, and inspire their team to overcome obstacles. Leaders with strong character exhibit empathy and compassion toward their team members. They genuinely care about the well-being of their employees and are willing to support them in times of need.

Your character will guide you as a leader in making ethical decisions. Leaders with strong character are less likely to compromise their principles for short-term gains, making them more likely to make decisions that benefit the greater good. Remember Harvey Weinstein? What comes to mind when you hear his name? Not his decades of success in Hollywood but the breach in character and morally wrong conduct. Leaders with strong character become positive role models for their team members. Their ethical behavior and principled approach inspire others to emulate similar values and behaviors, and this leads to them having long-term impact. Leaders with strong character focus on long-term success rather than short-term gains. They prioritize sustainable strategies and consider the broader impact of their decisions on the organization and its stakeholders.

The content of your character as part of leadership presence affects your capacity to lead. You must consistently work to build your character to lead effectively. If you have a character flaw in an area that affects your work significantly, then you have a capacity limitation in that area, and you must be cognizant of this and improve in that area.

CONFIDENCE

Confidence is a state of self-assurance and belief in one's abilities, skills, and judgment. It is an inner belief that you can tackle challenges, take risks, and navigate uncertainty with a positive outlook. Knowledge and acceptance of your identity, coupled with mastery, builds confidence.

One exhibition of a lack of confidence is poor or no decision-making. Confident leaders are more decisive and assertive in their decision-making. They trust their judgment and are willing to make tough choices, even in ambiguous or high-pressure situations. This clarity and decisiveness can lead to more efficient and effective decision-making processes. Confidence in the context of leadership presence affects your capacity because it shows up in your body language as well as how you speak.

The language of low confidence is negativity. Once, I facilitated a session on Clifton Strengths for some leaders in an agency. There was one participant who was extremely negative; he would shoot down any good ideas, saying it couldn't be done. Through powerful questioning, I found he was relatively new to this organization and had experienced events that shot his confidence in previous roles, so he had no optimism. Until he regained his confidence, he was performing at a very low capacity.

Confidence enhances a leader's communication and presence. Leaders who exude confidence are more likely to command attention and inspire trust and respect from their team members and stakeholders. The first ones usually have to work on their confidence because they hold back from taking risks. They fear judgment or punishment because no one has made them believe they can. I am telling you today, you can. I hope the insights you get from this book help you see and believe in your ability to lead. As your confidence grows in the context of leadership presence, your capacity will increase. You will be more willing to take calculated risks, while understanding that progress often requires stepping outside of comfort zones. This will empower you to explore innovative ideas and approaches, even if they come with some level of uncertainty.

CHARISMA AND ORATORY PROWESS

I define charisma as personal magnetism: Personal magnetism is the ability to draw people in with your words and energy. It is the ability to encounter others and leave them with a lasting impression. This is a certain grace and gift that is a huge asset for leadership in networking, public speaking, and building strategic relationships. Charisma is linked to oratory prowess, which is the exceptional skill in artistry in public speaking and delivering speeches. It is the ability to captivate, persuade, and inspire an audience through the effective use of language, gestures, and vocal techniques. Those with oratory prowess possess a commanding presence, and their speeches are often characterized by eloquence, clarity, and powerful delivery.

When you think of oratory prowess, think of Barack Obama. I think it was the singular thing that made him elected president. Whenever he spoke, he had a unique ability to combine fact, rhetorical devices, and emotional appeal to take his listeners on a journey to a promised land. He was the only politician to draw in the crowds just to hear his speeches. In fact, it was his speech at the Democratic National Convention on July 27, 2004, at the Fleet Center (now TD Garden) in Boston, when he was an Illinois State Senator running for the United States Senate, that catapulted him onto the national stage and laid the foundation for his future presidential campaigns. This shows you how the capacity you have with charisma and oratory prowess makes you a magnificent leader.

It is important to know that everyone has a natural proclivity for increased capacity in one area more than another. The goal is not to try to covet all components of leadership presence but realize what you have capacity for, areas you can focus on, build your leadership philosophy from, and lead effectively from. Things like charisma and public speaking may come naturally to certain personality types and natural talent, but leadership presence can be cultivated and grown across other components. Leadership presence is a prerequisite for public facing roles. Politicians, entrepreneurs, and public speakers require leadership presence to be successful. Leaders who are very public facing may not need to be strong in all components of leadership presence. The goal for you, the first one, is to know your capacity, hone it, and play in fields where you can leverage it to the fullest.

Here are some tips to help you strengthen your leadership presence:

1. **Work on your character:** If you have character flaws, be honest about them and develop the discipline to improve in those areas.
2. **Seek professional help:** Great leaders have coaches, therapists, and advisors, so don't be hesitant in seeking help to help improve your behavior.

3. **Practice public speaking:** Most people report that constant practice helps to quell the fear of public speaking; use meetings and opportunities with a friendly group to practice.
4. **Enroll in training:** There are courses available on effective communication and public speaking that can give you tips that will suit your personality type.
5. **See yourself as a brand:** Be intentional about the message you want people to have when they engage with you. Be intentional about your appearance, affiliations, social media content, and so on. All of these affect your brand and leadership presence.

TENACITY

Tenacity is simply the ability to stick to it; it is the ability to stay on task, irrespective of obstacles, challenges, and difficulties. It is another yardstick to measure your capacity as a leader. Tenacity speaks to your capacity to withstand storms, your ability to stay the course on the way to your destination and to continue to persevere, regardless of obstacles, roadblocks, or bad conditions. Sometimes, tenacity can be described in terms of stamina, so if you think about long-distance runners, for example, stamina and endurance are very critical, because the race is long, and they require energy to be released at intervals instead of a burst, like a sprint. Endurance and stamina speak to tenacity, and as a leader, it is important for you to understand your capacity when it comes to tenacity. You must understand how far you can go. This component of capacity differentiates leaders who are successful long term. If you study an industry and find industry leaders that have dominated the market for decades, they have tenacity.

Tenacity can also be called bandwidth. Bandwidth is the energy or mental capacity required to deal with a particular situation. Organizations define bandwidth in terms of staff strength, working capital, strategy, competitive advantage, partnerships. These strengths determine what opportunities the organization can leverage. As a leader, you need to know your strengths; we all have different strengths that are suitable for different situations. Some people have more bandwidth when it comes to people skills, while others have great strength with numbers. Other leaders are very technologically savvy, while some leaders are very good at building structures and systems. Tenacity is the ability to utilize strengths in ways that bring about impact and have the consistency and stamina to reach the goal.

How far can you go? What is your staying power? Leaders, presidents, and CEOs who have maintained relevance for extended periods of time have tenacity. Artists and actors who continue to deliver excellent performances for decades have tenacity. Tenacity is the ability to deliver results over time. When I think of tenacity, one name comes to mind: Nelson Mandela. There is no one else in modern history who demonstrated tenacity to accomplish his mission to the extent that he did with the level of personal sacrifice, suffering, and opposition he faced. He is a case study in tenacity. Tenacity is what makes people enter the history books.

Nelson Mandela's tenacity in fighting against apartheid in South Africa was deeply rooted in his unwavering commitment to justice, equality, and the belief that all people should be treated with dignity and respect. Despite facing numerous challenges, including imprisonment and opposition from the apartheid government, Mandela's determination to dismantle the unjust system remained steadfast. Several factors contributed to his resilience and unyielding spirit:

1. **Personal Conviction:** Mandela's personal experiences of witnessing the discrimination and oppression faced by the black population in South Africa fueled his determination to fight against apartheid. He believed passionately in the inherent equality of all people and was driven to create a more just society.

2. **Long-Term Vision:** Mandela had a clear long-term vision for a democratic and non-racial South Africa. He was not deterred by immediate setbacks or hardships but remained focused on the ultimate goal of dismantling apartheid and establishing a free and democratic nation.

3. **Moral Authority:** Mandela's principled stance against apartheid and his commitment to nonviolent resistance earned him moral authority both within South Africa and on the international stage. His strong moral standing inspired millions of people to join the struggle for freedom.

4. **Resilience and Perseverance:** Despite being imprisoned under harsh conditions on Robben Island for twenty-seven years, Mandela never wavered in his determination to fight for justice. He maintained his resilience and persevered through the darkest times, refusing to compromise his principles.

5. **Unity and Collaboration:** Mandela understood the power of unity and collaboration. He worked tirelessly to build alliances and partnerships both within South Africa and with international communities that supported the anti-apartheid movement.

6. **Negotiation and Compromise:** Mandela recognized the importance of negotiation and compromise in achieving political change. While he was unwavering in his pursuit of justice, he also understood the necessity of engaging in talks to bring about a peaceful transition.

7. **Global Solidarity:** The international anti-apartheid movement played a significant role in supporting Mandela and the struggle against apartheid. Global solidarity and pressure from the international community added weight to the fight for justice in South Africa.

8. **Courage and Sacrifice:** Mandela displayed remarkable courage and was willing to make personal sacrifices for the greater good of his country and its people. He endured immense personal hardship and risked his life for the cause he believed in.

9. **Public Support:** Mandela garnered significant public support both within South Africa and worldwide. The people's unwavering commitment to the anti-apartheid movement further bolstered his determination to continue the fight.

Nelson Mandela's tenacity to fight against apartheid in South Africa became a symbol of hope and resilience for oppressed communities around the world. His commitment to justice and equality, combined with his remarkable leadership and unwavering spirit, ultimately led to the dismantling of apartheid and the birth of a new democratic South Africa. Mandela's legacy continues to inspire generations to stand up against injustice and work for a more equitable and inclusive world. This is what tenacity can birth.

In determining your capacity level in terms of tenacity, if you were in battle, when would you wave the white flag? How far can you go when personal suffering is involved? Sometimes, it is difficult to assess because you don't know how far you can go until you are actually faced with situations, faced with failures, faced with challenges, faced with obstacles, and then you push yourself, and when you overcome those circles, it builds tenacity; however, every human being has a breaking point, and some people just have a natural ability or a greater ability to keep coming back. They go through difficulties, but they bounce back; they go through obstacles and failures, but they find the strength somehow. They have that inner strength that keeps fueling them, while other people go through something once or twice and they're done, and it doesn't come naturally for them to keep getting back up. It just takes a bit more for them to keep coming back up.

To understand tenacity further, let us use the analogy of a cheetah versus an antelope. The cheetah can go very fast for only a short period of time. The antelope also goes fast, not as fast as a cheetah, but can go fast for a longer period. Although the cheetah is faster than the antelope, the antelope is more tenacious because it can deliver results over a longer time. Leadership is about changing the status quo, blazing new trails, and creating new products, services, and solutions. These results do not happen overnight. Results take time, with consistent effort or application of strength. Leadership can be very challenging when you're leading a new initiative, starting a new product line, or leading people in a bureaucracy. There will be challenges, there will be difficulties, and it's important as a leader for you to have an awareness of your tenacity level. How far can you go? How much can you take and keep on course with the task?

We often hear from motivational speakers, never give up, never stop, but I want to challenge that premise because I believe as human beings, we all have limits, and in addition, I believe the mentality of "keep going at all costs" can cause you to fail. I say, never give up, as long as you have the capacity to continue. Of course, failure is never final, but that mentality to keep pushing past our limits and keep going, keep going, can be very detrimental. It can be counterproductive; we've seen burnout rates increase in the last couple of years. Stress and burnouts have been a major deterrent of productivity and effectiveness of leaders, and I think it is critical to have an awareness of how far you can go.

How much can you take? Do you know how many hits you can take before you have to pivot to something else? I'd like to introduce a concept called the sunk cost policy, a psychological phenomenon where we value an event or relationship or project or thing based on how much time and effort we have put into it, without consideration of results. Leadership produces results; leadership accomplishes goals. Tenacity is about effort, which is the application of strength in the right direction, with consistency and stamina.

One of the reasons leaders don't actualize their vision is they wrongly focus on only one aspect of tenacity. Direction without effort will yield nothing. Effort in the wrong direction will not produce a result. Effort in the right direction, without consistency over time, will not yield the full measure of the result. Great leaders always count the cost, always decide they are willing to pay the price for the result. Great leaders always conduct inventory of their tenacity level for every situation and task. Great leaders should also know what they are not meant to embark on. In military strategy, commanders conduct analysis of the terrain, consequences of actions, implications, and new arising issues before deciding on a course of action. As a great leader, it is okay to decide that some actions are not wise to embark on at a particular time because you don't have the tenacity to see it through to the desired result; it is okay to pivot when things are not working. Great leaders know when to cut their losses and pivot, regroup, re-strategize, and make changes.

Sticking to something even when it's not working and believing for the best makes us start to assess the results we're getting based on the sunk cost instead of actual impact. Therefore, we struggle to exit bad relationships, business deals, or partnerships or retire a product or initiative or program that is no longer effective. It is possible to put in very hard work and time in the wrong thing. It is possible to run speedily in the wrong direction. The right amount of effort in the right direction leads to impact. Leaders often focus on effort and intensity, and not direction or positioning. Solving a problem may require not doing more of the same thing; the solution may just be an adjustment in direction, such as changing the suppliers for your product, hiring someone else with a different skill set for the same role, moving into a different niche of the market, defining your services in more relatable terms.

On the other end of the spectrum, very little tenacity makes it really difficult to achieve goals and objectives because goals and objectives take time, effort, and strategy to materialize. There will be obstacles, and if you don't have tenacity, you'll quit at the very first sign of opposition or difficulty. It is your job as a leader to understand where you fall within the spectrum and if you need to build capacity around stamina and tenacity, or even if leadership is for you at all. I have met with people who say they see themselves as a very good number two or a wingman (or woman) because they don't want the responsibility of leadership, and I admire that. These people have great awareness of their capacity and know what is the best fit for them. You don't have to be the front-line leader to make an impact. You can lead from the sidelines and support the front-liner's vision. You can be the person the front-line leader needs to accomplish the mission. When it comes to tenacity, we can develop and build our capacity in these areas, but we need to be able to be honest and count the cost of being the one who knows the way, goes the way, and shows the way.

Counting the cost per time of what it will take for you to lead will guide how you appropriate all of the emotional and mental resources that go into staying tenacious, because tenacity requires patience. It requires physical, emotional, and mental stamina. It requires learning; it requires refueling, and all of these things are resources we possess, and so we need to know how many of those resources we have so we can properly apply them. That helps us assess how far we should go on a particular issue or project.

For example, one of the things I share with leaders I coach is, you don't exert the same amount of energy on every issue. Issues of higher importance or more consequential outcomes require more resources from you, so for example, if you are looking to launch a product that is going to be groundbreaking and has a very high barrier of entry to the market, that is going to require you to be more tenacious. It's going to require more resources, more physical stamina, more mental stamina, more patience, more fortitude, and more refueling to be able to bounce back from setbacks, but routine tasks do not require as much mental and emotional resources, so magnificent leaders are always aware of what they have in their energy cup; they steward their energy wisely.

What do you have in your energy cup? How much of it do you have, and how would you dispense that energy? The ability to manage mental, emotional, and physical resources as a human being, as a leader, speaks to your level of tenacity; it speaks to your staying power as a leader.

It affects your ability to have a long-lasting impact; now, for some industries, long lasting may not be applicable. For example, in the tech world, the model is to get in with an app or software, increase the user base, increase adoption, and sell. Most original founders of the popular apps we use today have sold their business. This type of market does not require high tenacity and intensity over time because there is a predetermined exit strategy, and the run time is short.

There are other situations that are ongoing, and results take longer to materialize. Some programs and projects take a long time to materialize and produce effects; things like social causes that require people to change their ways of thinking or challenge the status quo usually have a longer run time to mission accomplishment. This is the case, for example, with wars; they always take longer than originally anticipated. As the first one, it is not uncommon to underestimate how challenging the journey will be and what it will cost in terms of emotional and mental resources. This is simply because you don't know what you don't know.

My goal is to prepare you and make you aware of what it will take; doing great things is often a very long and hard journey with obstacles, failures, challenges, and unsolvable problems, and that's why a lot of people give up. There are very few people at the top, so tenacity is one of the essential pieces you need to consider in order to gauge your capacity as a leader, it's one thing to have ideas and goals and skills and gifts; it's another thing to have the staying power and make those things materialize. Tenacity is the difference between a dream and an outcome as a leader; you need to be aware of what it will take for you to get the outcomes you desire with your team, with your business, with your organization, and you need to be honest with yourself about whether you're willing to pay the price.

I sold real estate for ten years, and we were taught how to qualify a good buyer: A good buyer is ready, willing, and able. The ready piece speaks to buyers who are prepared and have done all the prerequisites for home buying; they've done their research, they know what neighborhood they want to live in, they know the home-buying process, and they have hired an agent. The willing part speaks to their internal drive and decision to buy a house. Willing buyers make an offer on a property they like; some people say they want to buy a house, but they're just riding around and viewing properties. They are not ready to commit. They are not willing to make that decision. The able piece means they have the money or have arranged financing to buy the property. Their credit is where it needs to be, and they have the money for the down payment.

When it comes to tenacity, you must ask if you are ready, willing, and able to do what it takes to see your vision all the way to the outcome? As human beings, our capacity is limited per time, but it's not finite, which means we can expand. We can grow; we can build capacity in the areas where there are gaps.

Here are some tips to build tenacity:

1. **Understand seasons and cycles:** Working with seasons and cycles will help you develop a rhythm of working with high intensity periods and low intensity periods so you have longer staying power.
2. **Self-care:** Understand what fuels you, and consistently plug into it. This will help you retain the stamina to push through difficult times.
3. **Enlist support:** Reframe the go-it-alone mentality. You don't personally have to handle all aspects of the job; empower your team so that you can delegate.
4. **Eliminate interferences:** Most leaders are nurturers, and so there is room for interference to deplete your energy level. Be intentional on what and who you give energy to. Some activities or relationships are good but not profitable. Stop unprofitable hard labor.

DOMAIN EXPERTISE

Seth Godin said, "Developing expertise or assets that are not easily copied is essential otherwise you're just a middleman." Great leaders in industry and business do hard things to set themselves apart on the issues.

Domain expertise simply means having a continuous working knowledge of the environment, trends, and stakeholder needs in your industry. This is another measure of your capacity as a leader. How much command do you have of the issues in your business and work environment? For example, to start up a cosmetic line, you must develop a working knowledge of the beauty industry, stakeholders and funders, and major shareholders; you must understand who the key players are. Having domain expertise means you know how things work with different business models that are out there for cosmetic companies; it means knowing the competitors and who their suppliers are. Your domain expertise means you know the regulations that govern the industry; you know the supply chain and the behaviors of your target market. You must know your target audience; you must know who you are speaking to with your product. You should know the answers to these questions about your target customers: What do they need? What is missing in the market that will appeal to them? What are their fears? What are the aspirations?

This is what domain expertise is, and domain expertise only comes through continuous learning, experience, and mentoring. This is a key metric of capacity for leadership. You must commit to maintaining domain expertise where you lead. Whether you are a champion in social causes for a particular demographic, or you are advocating for changes in climate policy, the economy, gender issues, or mental health issues, the depth and breadth of your knowledge, understanding, and application of the subject matter denotes your level of capacity to lead. People say you don't have to be an expert in a field to lead in it; you just need to hire experts. That is not completely true. As a leader, you must know the work to hire the right experts, and you must have command of that industry to lead effectively, but I agree you don't need to have the deepest expertise in all the technical areas of your organization.

In this context, the word *expert* means relevant knowledge; you must have working knowledge, deep knowledge of the issues around what your leadership cause is. You cannot lead effectively in an environment where you are novice. You may start as a novice but be intentional about committing to gaining relevant knowledge and wisdom; otherwise, your influence will be stifled. When people pick up that you lack domain expertise, it is an opening for them to undermine your leadership. You must continue to increase domain expertise to maintain influence. It requires intentionality and consistency. Learning is leadership. If you cannot learn, you cannot lead, so therefore, your capacity to learn is a metric to measure your capacity as a leader.

Continuous learning is part of key leadership competency, so when it comes to domain expertise, you can get it one of two ways. One way of gaining domain expertise is formal education and traditional work experience: going to college, getting a bachelor's or master's degree, gaining credentials or certification, and industry-specific trainings. Some industries require formal training and even licenses to work in, like CPAs and healthcare professionals; working in an industry with large or small employees, you can do internships and take job training programs.

Then there is the informal learning process, which I call the school of life; this learning process comprises knowledge that comes from failure, suffering, curiosity, reading, traveling, and experiencing different cultures. This is experience; when you read books, you learn. When you study biographies and go outside the formal educational system, you get more information. We live in the information age, so there's no shortage of information anywhere. I want to speak specifically to young people because I believe they have been sold this idea that you can achieve domain expertise based on informal education alone. The challenge with that is, with informal education, you seek out the information, learn it, and test yourself. With formal education, you have been tested by an educational body that can verify you have the knowledge. If you want to rely on informal education alone and want to lead, you must have people who have endorsed you and attest you have the knowledge you say you have. Also, young people, you cannot lead with talent alone. You must have a command of the issues and the environment. Do not buy into the glorification of ignorance that is taking place. Every great thing you want to do exists within a system you didn't create. You must master the system. Learn how it works, who it favors, what loopholes exist so you know how to move within it.

If you don't understand how things work, and if you don't have domain expertise, you may be able to start and gain some level of success, but it will quickly come crashing down. We see this a lot with athletes or musicians who quickly rise to fame and success without understanding their industry or business of their work. If you read the stories of winners of shows like *American Idol* or *America's Got Talent*, you'll find some winners were not able to successfully convert their wins to successful careers; they didn't learn the business of show business. For example, they didn't know when you get a record deal, there are certain things you have to do to be able to maintain it, and there is always the fine print; they didn't know they needed to hire lawyers and accountants to protect their interests.

I watched an interview with Michael Vick, the former quarterback, who had a very successful career in football and was on his way to being a Hall of Fame NFL player but made some bad decisions as a result of not having domain expertise of the business environment and industry. He became involved in dog fighting and was arrested and found guilty of illegal commercial activities. He ended up serving time in jail. He is an excellent football player but lacked domain expertise of the NFL business. He didn't have the business infrastructure in place to prevent him from making a costly mistake that would end his career. Having domain expertise helps you make good judgment calls, and that is a hallmark of leadership.

Expertise is critical, so young people, if you want to lead, get a command of the issues and a thorough understanding of the environment. You don't have to use the traditional means of education; you don't have to have a degree, but you need to have a command of the issues. You have to have domain expertise because this lends to your influence and your ability to make good decisions and have sound judgment. You need to understand the interoperability of different issues. Simply put, you need to know, if I do this, what will happen? If I move this way, what will happen to the rest of my brand? Domain expertise contributes significantly to your capacity. It is very interesting to watch leaders who have no clue what they're doing, new bosses who know nothing about the terrain. If they don't invest in relationships with key players and learn the terrain or environment quickly, they sink.

A recent US president was elected to office because people wanted something new and something fresh, but the man had no understanding of how government worked. It's not enough to just say you have the gift, the skill, or the ability to do the job; you need to understand the work itself. If you're going to lead in government, you need to understand how the government works; if you're going to lead in a nonprofit sector, you need to understand how the nonprofit sector works. If you're going to lead in tech, you need to understand the tech industry. Leaders study to show they are accomplished. Leadership is learning; leadership is continuous learning because domain expertise is required. It is required when it comes to making decisions, crafting strategies, and preparing for the unexpected; hiring the right team with domain expertise comes into a big play. When it comes to your effectiveness, your ability to do the right things at the right time as a leader is critical. Great leaders read, great leaders observe, great leaders are committed to learning.

Your ability to learn and continually gain domain expertise is a capacity factor for leadership; gaining domain expertise takes intentionality, it takes consistency, and it takes humility. Magnificent leaders know what they don't know and know they don't know a lot of things. That's where domain expertise starts, and so they embrace failure because they know it's there to teach them. They listen to wise counsel and practice deep, active listening because they know they need to hear from people. They prioritize opportunities to get new insights and look at things from a fresh perspective. Magnificent leaders study history because there is nothing new under the sun.

There is this new trend of trashing tradition, ignoring history, and demonizing knowledge; no wonder we have a leadership crisis in the world. We have unseasoned folks at the helm of affairs, calling the shots that affect millions of people. People say bad knowledge can be used to manipulate people; however, ignorance kills. Leaders like Nelson Mandela, Barack Obama, and Martin Luther King had a command of the issues and were experts at their day jobs. Mandela was an expert lawyer who knew the deadly consequences of apartheid; that is why his words carried weight. Obama is a skilled lawyer who can explain how a bill in conceived, birthed, and grown into a program to help the American public. Therefore, he was able to pass the Affordable Care Act; he had domain expertise in how government works. Martin Luther King was a preacher and a seasoned attorney, so he knew where the loopholes were in the law as regards civil rights.

When it comes to your capacity as a leader, knowledge is a powerful tool; the right application of knowledge is wisdom, and that also speaks to domain expertise, so you get knowledge from learning, but you gain wisdom from observing and watching and feeling. Domain expertise takes time; young people, you want to lead? Do what you need to do now to have a command of the issues. That domain expertise is critical to your ability to influence and get the attention of others; it takes time. There's a lot of pressure for young people to step out when they are not yet prepared. And yes, there is some learning that takes place as you step out, but you have to be intentional that even as you step out and continue to learn, you have to sharpen your sword.

Young people, give yourself time to gain expertise about the issues you're passionate about. Passion without knowledge is noise. True success does not happen overnight. Some industries are more stringent when they measure domain expertise; as a leader, you need to know who is considered an expert. What does expertise look like for your industry? Look at the people who are winning; what do they have? You know what degrees they have? What work experience do they have? Work experience is also part of domain expertise. People often reach out to me about wanting to do government contracting, and I tell them, if you want to get government contracts, go work for a contractor so you understand what goes on behind the scenes, how the contracts are sourced, what the company must do to maintain compliance with federal regulations, how contracts are priced. That's what the job is. The job is training. When I hear people say they don't want to work for someone else but want to start their own company when they have no knowledge of the field, I chuckle. You cannot cheat experience. If you want to have a successful business in an industry, you should get a job or volunteer in that industry and learn the innerworkings, rather than flying blind and starting a business and learning the hard way, with blood, sweat, and tears and probably debt, making costly mistakes. You choose which way you want to learn, but either way, you must gain the knowledge. You can learn by being taught or the hard way through painful experiences. Your call.

The most common way to gain domain expertise outside traditional learning is mentoring. Mentoring is leveraging the knowledge and expertise of others through a formal or informal relationship. While mentoring is a great way to develop domain expertise, it should not be a substitution for personal commitment to continuous learning. Effective leadership requires commitment to continuous learning through experience and education. This is because relying only on mentoring can lead to identity distortion.

You want to extract lessons from mentors, not be a duplicate of them. You and your mentor have different identities and purposes; that makes it unwise for you to be a copy of them. I chuckle when I hear people say they want to be the next Kim Kardashian or Elon Musk; I ask them, do you have the same genetic, psychological, and physical makeup as them? Do you have the same background and exposure/privileges as them? Is your purpose the same as theirs? I think there is room for us to learn lessons about principles of leadership from mentors' stories, whether formal or informal. However, you must maintain your own originality and identity because that is where your own superpower lies.

Domain expertise increases your credibility as a leader. Credibility is when people believe you. People need to trust you can do the work you were tapped for. A lack of domain expertise undermines your credibility with your team, especially if you are unable to provide solutions for them as their leader. Credibility is very important in leadership; people follow you because they believe you know the right way to go. They believe you can deliver results.

Having credibility means you possess the qualities and knowledge people who follow you need. Domain expertise lends you credibility. This is a big capacity issue we see in today's world, where everyone is an expert on something by watching YouTube; people don't really want to take the time to study the issues, to study history. People no longer study trends and factors that affect any environment, whether it's a business, a program, a technology, or financial factors. People don't want to study their target market and learn behavior patterns of customers; they just want to jump into business and become a millionaire in ninety days. This is why I don't believe in multiple streams of income in different industries because it takes time to develop domain expertise in a space. Instead, you should build on your business, expanding from one concept to a related concept or industry.

Knowledge and insight boost your credibility. People follow leaders they believe have the answers, deep knowledge of the issues. For example, if you had a serious heart condition, would you want a cardiologist who is fresh out of residency? No, I don't think so. You'd want someone with years of experience who has treated several patients with similar conditions as the one you face with successful past performance.

I'll never forget what one of my mentors told me after I said I was interested in moving from clinical case management to management consulting. She said, "Maria, no one will pay you as a consultant to practice on them; you need to get an MBA." Her advice led me to enroll in an MBA program and an executive coaching program in Georgetown University. The knowledge I gained from these programs added depth to my experience in my career that I would not have gotten otherwise. In the consulting field, there are several methodologies, frameworks, and theories that experts use to provide solutions to clients. As a consultant, being well rounded in best practices helps you maintain value in your career, so every year, I invest in continuous learning to keep up with cutting-edge best practices in the field. I attend conferences, read books, and listen to podcasts. I am constantly sharpening my sword, so I have the answers that are asked of me in my leadership journey.

Domain expertise comes from a commitment to continuous learning; it's not just a matter of getting the degree or getting the certification and putting the checkmark or different letters behind your name. Domain expertise is a commitment to continuous learning because the facts are constantly changing; history is constantly being made. Trends are springing up every day, so to have domain expertise, you need to be continually open and look for the information that will give you situational awareness and the ability to provide solutions to the problems in your organization and for your customers.

This capacity marker is often overlooked. Leaders who don't study never have the answers and don't know where to look for them. This is your responsibility as a leader; you need to have the answers or know where to get them. If you're not increasing your knowledge, at some point in time, the environment will either put you out of business or make you irrelevant. Leaders without domain expertise often make very poor decisions. They are often lightweight and end up being irrelevant and inconsequential. Domain expertise speaks to relevancy as well as credibility. I have observed that when leaders lack domain knowledge, they defer to others to execute their core responsibilities. Yes, there is a place for delegation, but as a leader, you should be competent enough to handle your core duties.

If you watch the news, political pundits, consultants, and experts are often brought in to discuss various subjects. Most times, all have one thing in common: a command of the issues. When topics of national security are being discussed, the expert brought in is usually a former senior National Security Agency official who has a domain knowledge of the issues and can provide insight to what the breaking news is about. When an election is taking place, the network show hosts bring in former successful campaign officials for governors or presidents to offer their perspective as experts. When people want to learn something they don't know, they look to the experts.

I always tell leaders I coach you never want to lead in a space where you do not have the ability or resources to grow your domain expertise because you would always lack credibility and relevance. Sometimes, we see organizations sabotage their managers and emerging leaders when they throw them into new environments and then don't give them the tools they need to continuously learn and grow.

Here are some tips to help you increase domain expertise:

1. **Have a beginner's mindset**: Most people who are experts in their fields have a beginner's mindset. They approach life with the humility to learn daily from everything, so they know so much. A know-it-all mentality will leave you with a narrow and shallow perspective.
2. **Develop a culture of continuous learning**: Invest in learning programs, conferences, events.
3. **Surround yourself with smart people**: Ignorance is contagious; maintain social distance from it. As a magnificent leader, if you don't have an answer, you should be within two degrees of separation from someone who does.

Your capacity as a leader is not stagnant. You can grow capacity in any area you desire, and you have limits as a leader. These two statements are true at the same time. You can grow capacity in intuition, leadership presence, tenacity, and domain expertise. Personality types make it easier for some folks to have more capacity in certain areas. For example, if you're a social and charismatic person, leadership presence may come easier to you. If you are more of a knowledge seeker, a brainiac, someone who fancies intellect, you may notice you grasp information easily, and increased domain expertise will come easier to you. Then, if you're someone who's tough, stubborn, and defiant, the tenacity piece will come easier to you.

Your focus in leading yourself is to continually evaluate and conduct inventory of where you are with your capacity, in relation to what you want to take on and the goals you want to achieve. This is really a marker of knowing yourself, knowing where you are, and being honest about where you are along these different dimensions of capacity. Intuition, leadership presence, tenacity, and domain expertise are very broad topics. These topics encompass many leadership competencies. It is your responsibility as a leader to constantly conduct inventory on where you are on the scale in these three areas in relation to what is required for your leadership journey.

In the context of defining and rating capacity, I want to use the flow of energy as an analogy. Energy from a scientific perspective is defined as the physical, mental, emotional, and spiritual strength (ability to exert force) and power (strength plus speed) you use to do work. Your energy determines your capacity. Energy can be defined in multiple dimensions (types), and it exists in different forms. Energy is never lost; it only changes from one form to another. Consider intuition, leadership presence, tenacity, and domain expertise as different forms or types of energy. As a leader, you are always exerting energy on something, and depending on the specific issue or industry, one type of energy may be more suitable for the job. Your ability to direct that energy, increase or decrease intensity, and plug into source to refuel that energy is a skill to be developed. Simply put, it is your job to manage your cup. Your capacity is what is in your cup. What does it mean to have a full cup? Think about it in terms of percentage; 100 percent is a full cup, the optimum energy state or optimum capacity for your role as a leader. You get to define what a full cup looks like to you. I would say a full cup looks like being up to the task, having the solutions and support of a team, having sound judgment and focus, and lacking distractions. When your cup is full, you're able to carry out daily functions, withstand the shock of unplanned events, and display mental agility; you are resourceful and physically able to navigate complex, volatile, fast-changing, and ambiguous issues, which you will often face in leadership.

Additionally, capacity is not equal to access. Your capacity to execute a function should not give immediate access to everyone who has a need for that function or who can use that capacity in every circumstance. As the first one, you must learn to direct your energy in the most purposeful manner. I always tell leaders I coach that as you grow in leadership, your words, actions, and decisions should be so weighty and potent that you only need to use them sparingly. Meaning that you are responsible for managing who has access to your capacity. There must be an intake process to qualify who has access to what you have the capacity to do. For example, when you take a job, that work will require you to use up your capacity, so that job better be in service to a cause that matters to you, advance your career goals, and compensate you commensurately.

It is also your responsibility to steward your seasons as a leader. Sometimes, you may be in a season of expending energy, stamina, and knowledge, and then at other times, you're in a season of refueling, transitioning, and pivoting. Understand when you need to push hard on activities or step back and observe and learn. You need to ask yourself, are you in a season where you can go a little bit harder on some of your pressing goals because you feel you have the strength and tenacity to do so? In the beginning phases of your leadership journey, you need to focus on really building domain expertise, so you have credibility and relevance in the space where you're leading. As you become more experienced as a leader, your intuition comes more to the forefront, and you rely on it more as your energy form of choice. Also, a relevant question you should ask yourself is, do you want to be the public face of your business or organization? If you do, you must be prepared to demonstrate strong leadership presence. If not, you may need to hire someone who will be more public-facing so that you do not need to do so much of the outward facing leadership activities (if leadership presence is difficult for you).

Taking constant inventory of your capacity demonstrates self-management, which is one of the components of emotional intelligence. It also requires self-awareness, which is another component of emotional intelligence; these are critical pillars of leadership, and developing these capacities will help you provide solutions, be innovative, and produce results.

3

LEADERSHIP PHILOSOPHY

Once you are clear on your identity and capacity as a leader, you must then craft your own leadership philosophy and lead by it. Leadership philosophy is your own way of influencing the values or causes you believe in, what people should expect from you when they encounter you as a leader, and what you will not engage in as a leader.

In determining your leadership philosophy, ask yourself this question: What kind of leader do I want to be? There is a lot of information out there about different leadership styles; my perspective is, there's no right or wrong or good or bad leadership style. There are seven common leadership styles: autocratic, pacesetting, transformational, coaching, democratic, conciliatory, and delegative:

Autocratic Leadership: This is usually authoritarian, very structured, and very focused on results. Beneficial for highly regulated industries and when there is a short time frame for action. A major drawback is that leadership authority can be easily abused by an autocratic leader.

Pacesetting Leadership: This is leading by example, highly energetic leaders who push their teams hard but roll up their sleeves and work with them. Beneficial when deadlines must be met with minimal resources. The drawback of this style is the burnout of staff and increased mistakes in a very fast-paced and high-stress environment.

Transformational Leadership: Visionary leaders lead by empowering and developing teams; beneficial for navigating change and spurring growth in an organization. A major drawback is leaders can be too lofty with goals and may sacrifice day-to-day performance.

Coaching Leadership: These leaders focus on helping team members uncover and utilize their potential. This leadership style is popular in the sports industry. This style is time consuming and can become segmented only to team members who benefit from it.

Democratic Leadership: Democratic leaders are persuasive and focus on participation and consensus. Very popular in government settings, where decisions affect the general population. This style boosts creativity and engagement but can create delays in action and bottlenecks in decision-making.

Conciliatory Leadership: These leaders lead by making people feel good, appealing to the needs and senses of team members and focusing on harmony. This style is effective when something has gone wrong, and a leader needs to right the ship. A major con is that team members can manipulate the leader and stifle mission accomplishment.

Delegative Leadership: In this style of leadership, team members solve problems on their own and are challenged to take responsibility. This style is beneficial when you have a diverse portfolio as a leader and also helps organizations scale and do more. Drawback is dip in quality of work with team members are not well trained and conflicts among team members.

Different styles of leadership are more appropriate for certain situations, environments, and organization types. Some leaders prefer a combination of two or three styles and are flexible enough to use other styles when a situation warrants it.

For example, the democratic leadership style is necessary in the US federal government because there are laws in place that mandate the inclusion of employees in actions. In fact, the US government has an entire agency, the Equal Employment Opportunity Commission, that enforces these laws and provides recourse for employees who feel their leaders do not comply. Other industries like healthcare are heavily regulated; an autocratic leadership style is necessary to ensure that protocols and regulations are followed because deviation from protocol can mean the difference between life and death of a patient. However, in a healthcare setting, a magnificent leader can balance the autocratic style with a facilitative approach to ensure that employees' needs are addressed; this keeps morale high.

As another example, a transformational leader of a technology company may allow the space for employees to be creative and inspired, combining her approach with a pacesetting style during a new product launch to meet different demands. When it comes to style, there is not a one-size-fits-all approach; there is no right or wrong style. Every leadership style has its pros and cons and appropriate use. Your goal in leading yourself is knowing the most appropriate style for your personality, team, and organization environment. Also, it is important to note that when everything is going well, your leadership style may be different from how you lead during a crisis. During times of crisis, or when you have an urgent deadline that must be met, a commanding leadership style is necessary; other times, a conciliatory leadership style is important if your team is working on social issues that speak more to the soul of people or pull on people's emotions and feelings. People in the foster care or case management space often have to use this style.

Beyond your style, your leadership philosophy is the combination of styles you use for different situations, what you believe in, and how people should engage with you. Your leadership philosophy denotes how you lead. It is your personal doctrine for leadership.

For example, US presidents often show their leadership philosophy by how they assemble their cabinet and their stand on social issues, the economy, and foreign policy. While the Constitution confers their powers, it is their personal leadership philosophy that drives how they lead. This leadership is critical in the governing of nations. Institutions, rule of law, and public sentiments are all guardrails for the sovereignty of a nation, but the personnel at the helm of affairs matters because their leadership philosophy determines how they lead.

For example, let's examine the foreign policy doctrines of two previous US presidents. The Obama foreign policy doctrine emphasized a more measured and cooperative approach to international affairs, with a focus on diplomacy, multilateralism, and promoting democratic values. It aimed to restore America's standing as a respected global leader while tackling global challenges in a collaborative manner.

The Bush doctrine represented a significant departure from previous US foreign policy approaches and signaled a more assertive and interventionist stance, especially in the context of combating terrorism and promoting democracy. It shaped US foreign policy throughout George W. Bush's presidency and had a lasting impact on subsequent administrations' approach to national security and international affairs.

From these two examples, you see a sharp contrast in the leadership philosophy of both leaders, one a more measured, collaborative approach to foreign policy and the other a more interventionist approach, signaled by the war on terror.

As an emerging leader, one of the first things you need to work on is crafting your leadership philosophy. At AMA Consulting, we design leadership development programs for federal agency leaders. We help leaders work on their Leadership Development Plans (LDPs), in which they set up goals for themselves in competencies they want to develop during and after the program. In our cornerstone exercise, leaders develop their leadership philosophy and present it to their cohort members. Your leadership philosophy is your own constitution of how you lead, your fundamental principles and doctrines of how you operate. Magnificent leaders define their leadership philosophy based on their identity and capacity. Most of us are conditioned and influenced so much by mentors and role models that we just copy how they lead. While it is okay to be inspired by others, learn from them, and be motivated by them, we cannot reach our highest level of performance as copycats.

Your role models and mentors lead the way they do because of who they are and their capacity. You can be inspired by them to chart your own leadership course and lead in your own way. Therefore, you must be clear on your identity, clear on the things that matter to you, things that keep you up at night, things you are passionate about. You must be clear on your spiritual, psychological, and physical makeup. You must be clear on your capacity: your natural gift talents, your tendencies, your proclivities, your strengths, and your weaknesses, and your leadership philosophy should be based on that.

Your leadership philosophy puts it all together. It is the manual for how you will use your resources to lead. In determining your leadership philosophy, ask yourself, what do you believe about the work you want to do? What are you going to do with all your resources? What do you want to achieve? What is your role as a leader? What will you not accept when you lead? This is your creed.

A *creed* is defined as what you believe, what you stand for, how you operate; the same thing with the Constitution, it's like your rulebook. Your leadership philosophy is your rulebook, so your leadership philosophy should include your values, what you believe. You should also include what people should expect when they engage with you, and finally, your leadership philosophy should include nonnegotiables, the things you will not stand for or tolerate.

Remember the famous quote that "if you stand for nothing, you'll fall for anything"? What are your leadership philosophies? What do you stand for? How do you work? It is your responsibility as a leader to establish the rules of engagement in your leadership journey. This is a huge component of leading self. Most times, the first ones do not know that this is their responsibility and so do not take the time to craft their leadership philosophy, and they get upset when people do not respond to them the way they want.

For example, the constitution is the foundation or belief system a country is founded on. In the US, our belief system is based on the values of life, liberty, and the pursuit of happiness. That is why people come here; they gravity toward these values. They know if they come here, they can pursue happiness; they will be truly free to live the life they want. It is the only country in the world that offers this basic promise that every human being wants. That is why there are people here from all over the world. Your leadership philosophy will make people who believe in the same thing gravitate toward you.

The general cornerstone of your leadership philosophy should not change; however, your leadership philosophy can be amended as you grow and evolve as a leader. As you lead in different spaces, your style may change, but your values and what you stand for as a leader should not. It is very important that people know what to expect when they encounter you. It builds your brand and your reputation as a leader.

I invite you at this point to put everything we have discussed in the previous two chapters together. See your identity and capacity as the tools you have been handed to build a house; your leadership philosophy is how you use the tools and what tool you use for what part of the job. Your leadership philosophy should address the people you're going to lead. From your leadership philosophy, one should be able to profile your followers.

Leaders often spend a lot of time trying to convert people, persuade them, coerce them to come on board and join their vision. If you just focus on defining your creed and following it, acting out daily, and consistently being who you say you are in your leadership philosophy, your people will naturally gravitate toward you. Your work is to consistently live out what you believe and use your own tools; over time, your brand and reputation will establish your following.

Here is my leadership philosophy and how I came up with it:

As a leader, I use the transformational leadership style because I am very visionary, and I want to do great things with lasting impact. I always have a legacy at the forefront of my mind. In my role as CEO, I function with the autocratic style because my business is heavily regulated by federal rules and extremely competitive. With my employees, I employ a coaching style because I believe every human being is inherently whole, creative, and configured for greatness. When you engage with me, expect excellence, integrity, diligence, and compassion. These are the values I live by. I appreciate direct communication, and I do not entertain lies. I am willing to tolerate everything but something that is untrue. This is my leadership philosophy.

You can see how my leadership philosophy is set, even though I implore various leadership styles in different contexts. In crafting your leadership philosophy, give yourself the flexibility to adopt an environment where you may lead and apply your creed to each environment. For example, you can't lead in an environment of command and control like the military and have a flexible leadership philosophy. Military personnel are trained to follow orders. As a leader in the military, your philosophy should be different from a leader in a global nonprofit that is fighting climate change. The responsibility of developing your leadership philosophy is yours. It will help you figure out environments where you are likely to be most successful.

Here are some tips to craft your leadership philosophy:

1. **Take personality and psychometric assessments:** This will help you know your strengths and best suited style of leadership for your personality type.

2. **Build your leadership philosophy from what you believe in:** First-time leaders often decide how they lead based on what their organization says is effective. How you lead must be aligned to what you believe.

3. **Write it down:** Spend some time summarizing your core beliefs, what people should expect from you, and what you will not tolerate; write it on paper, don't just keep it as head knowledge.

4. **Tell people about it:** Make it a habit and practice to weave in your leadership philosophy into introductions and conversation so that you set the standard for how people engage with you.

4

WHAT DO YOU WANT TO DO?

VISION

In leading yourself, once you accept your identity, know your capacity, and define your leadership philosophy, you must then draw your vision. I use the word "draw" intentionally because your vision is a picture. It is that imaginative concept of the ideal state you want to achieve. When I coach leaders, I tell them their vision starts from where they are and goes to where they want to be. To be clear on your vision, ask the following questions: What is on your radar? What are you responsible for? What are you trying to do? How is it different from what currently exists? What ground are you trying to cover? What are you trying to create? What are you trying to do that has not been done before (or has not been done the way you plan to do it)? What does this new picture look like? What is the size of the picture? What are the colors, attributes, definitions? What and who does this picture appeal to? I define *vision* as painting a picture, per time, of the future you want to see when you get there.

It can become difficult to paint a picture of what you have not yet seen or experienced if you cannot connect it to what you are responsible for now. Today, it will be difficult to get cues of what that future picture looks like. This is another challenge the first ones have; they are often detached from their present in pursuit of the future, not knowing that the vision is a picture of the present in the future. If you get this, you will appreciate every stage, process, detour, setback, and triumph. A lot of very visionary people find it difficult to celebrate milestones and wins; sometimes, they don't even realize when their vision is manifesting because they are so caught up in the future. Vision requires the clarity of our mind's eye. We have to see the present and the future in the picture.

The camera that takes a snapshot of that picture is your mind. One of the greatest powers of the mind is to capture a picture per time of the future you want to create. This is why you must nurture your mind as a leader and be intentional about how you use your mind. You must guard your mind from messages and pictures that do not align with the vision you want and feed your mind with data, content, and pictures that give more definition to your vision.

Your vision is not a wish. A wish is just a fancy thought of what you'd like to see or have. A vision is a picture. Leaders must see this picture clearly first so that they can skillfully describe it to others. The picture quality of your vision will depend on the quality of your mind space and mind eyesight. Just like a more sophisticated camera captures clearer and sharper images, a more sophisticated mind captures a clearer and sharper vision.

As the first one, please understand that you oversee your mind space; you decide what gets in and what to take out. While you have default features in your mind from genetics, you get to decide how to use those features; you decide what colors, drawings, and images you want in your mind library to build your vision.

Have you ever tried to add a picture or a document to an email? The first step is to browse your computer files (library) for available images on your computer. If the image you want is not on the computer, you cannot add it. That is exactly how visioning works. Most people just repeat what others say or use lofty words or recite a wish as a vision. But that is not a vision. A vision is a picture downloaded from your mind from existing images in your mental library. So, if the image does not yet exist in your mental library, you cannot envision it.

Your picture or vision is a core consideration when you carry out the daily tasks of leadership. For example, every day when I set out to work,

I have the picture of my vision in mind, and it guides me. I am conscious that I am painting that picture with every decision I make and action I take. For me, a big piece of my leadership philosophy is doing great things with my family and business; my core value of excellence enables me to carry out this vision and attract employees who can execute it. I have never been interested in anything mediocre or average. I've always believed you can get by with just surviving, but survival is never the goal. In any role I'm in or any environment where I lead, the picture I paint is to do great things, and "great" means grand, superior, over the top, the best of the best, high excellence, magnificence, something that changes the landscape in a meaningful way, something that makes a mark and is defining, something that makes an impact. In colors, this vision is very bright; orange is my favorite color, signifying visible light, energy, optimism, and fieriness.

This is a core piece of my vision; in everything I do, I want it to be grand, and I develop leaders who also want to do great things, leaders who want to do things that matter on a large scale, things that move the needle on core issues, regardless of the environment or the program or the cause they work on. You can see how my values and my vision come together in my leadership philosophy. With my leadership philosophy so clear and articulate, if you're a coaster and just want to do the bare minimum, we are not going to be aligned. You're probably not going to want to follow me; you're probably going to see me as harsh or too demanding. I attract people who are optimistic, energetic, and always willing to shake things up. I attract people who can do hard things and can fight under water because this is what my vision demands. It is important because you need to articulate your vision as a leader, so the right people follow you.

One of the challenges first-time leaders face is having the courage to let people know how to engage with them. First-time leaders often cede the responsibility of engagement with their followers to the environment or to chance. You decide who is attracted to you and how they engage with you. As a leader, you are not for everyone, and your value as a leader does not apply or appeal to everyone. You have a specific niche of people to build, transform, and lead. It is your responsibility to know who you are called to lead. Jesus is the best example of a leader I have. Matthew 15:20–28 records the story of the Syrophoenician woman whose daughter was possessed by a demon. She knew Jesus could heal her daughter; Jesus had what she needed.

She approached Jesus audaciously to plead for healing for her daughter, and Jesus gives a chilling response to her in Matthew 15: "I was commissioned by God and sent only to the lost sheep of the house of Israel."

Wow. Healing was the cornerstone of Jesus's ministry. He had the power to do it, but here he is saying to her, "My value is not for you". You are not a part of the core constituency I lead. Jesus was sent to a particular group of people. Even with all his gifts, anointing, power, and wisdom, he targeted a particular group of people. The story goes on to show that through the woman's faith and persistence, she got Jesus to widen his scope and reach to include her. This is significant because those of us who are not part of the lost sheep of the house of Israel have access to Jesus through faith. As a leader, you must have your core constituency you are assigned to lead, and a process of including others who don't have the characteristics of your core constituents as followers. If you are not intentional about this as a first-time leader, people will abuse your gift and not appreciate your value, and you will not be effective.

Articulating your leadership philosophy helps you define your core followers. You must articulate how you show up in situations, what people should expect when they engage with you, and what you expect from the people who follow you. You should also know what you expect from them. You have probably heard the saying "You teach people how to treat you." This is true because leaders, especially the first ones, are susceptible to abuse, misuse, and betrayal. For example, your leadership philosophy should include how you communicate: Are you a direct communicator, or do you communicate with cues? Are you someone who is tough or casual? Are you prompt or lax with time? Are you a plan-ahead type of leader or a let's see how it goes leader?

Most times, your environment, industry, nature of work, or conditioning affects how you show up, but people need to know that upfront. That way, they know what they're getting into when they decide to come on board with your vision. In turn, you need to let people know what you expect so you ensure you are attracting the right followers who will help you accomplish your goal. Your job as a leader is to harness the right people to help you accomplish your goal. Going back to the story of the Syrophoenician woman, healing her daughter was within Jesus's ability, and it would be nice to heal her daughter. After all, it will garner more fame and popularity for Jesus, and the girl will be free to live without demonic oppression, but it was not within the scope of Jesus's main goal, which was to fulfill the prophesy of the Messiah for Israel. This is why he initially said 'no' to her. As a leader, you constantly must choose between doing the "good thing" and the "goal thing"; some actions may be good for you to do but will not get you to your goal. While you can do good things on exception, you want to make the habit of doing goal things, so you achieve your mission. Having your leadership philosophy helps keep your vision front and center.

Once you have your vision, the picture, you need to be clear on the work itself. Where do you need to go to make that picture real?

ASSIGNMENT

Your assignment is simply what you have a passion for. It is what you always gravitate toward. It could be a cause that is dear and near to your heart. Your assignment ignites a fire in you that will not stop burning until you act on it. For me, leadership development is my assignment. I feel most fulfilled when I'm coaching, training, or supporting leaders. I am passionate about all aspects of leadership development: coaching, training, character development, growth, maturity, and leadership competencies. You should see the smile on my face as I write this. It gives me joy just to talk about it. I gravitate to content on anything related to character development, relationship management, strategy, and vision. This is my life's work. I know this like I know my name. When I speak on leadership, it comes naturally to me. I embody the work. Your assignment as a leader is what you have set out to do. I define *assignment* as your life's work.

Goals and objectives must be tied to your overall assignment. Vision is a picture, but assignment is your life's work. In thinking of your assignment, all the jobs you've held either prepare you for your assignment or reveal your assignment. Your life experiences also reveal your assignment and build your capacity to fulfill your assignment. The process of working out your assignment is what brings the ultimate fulfillment as a leader. These days, people want to be what others consider to be successful. People do things they think will make them get money or fame. But we've seen successful, rich people commit suicide due to a lack of fulfillment. Some people have made society's definition of fulfillment theirs and are stretching themselves to achieve it, when it is not even their own assignment.

Sometimes, parents unknowingly fall into this trap; raising kids is part of establishing a family, but that is not the totality of your assignment. The gifts you've been given and the experience you have gained in life are for a purpose. There is a gap in the earth you are assigned to work on. Your assignment is your watch post. It is what you've been given the authority, capacity, and resources to create and engineer. Leaders who know their assignment and stay consistently in their place and on their post exude confidence and influence.

Your assignment may not be your job.

Your assignment is not what other people tell you to do or expect you to do.

Your assignment may not be your parents' assignment.

Your assignment may not be popular in culture.

Your assignment may not be easy and comfortable.

Your assignment may not have a definition in the culture or environment where you were raised.

The revelation of your assignment only comes to you. Others may confirm it, but the revelation of it and working of it must be defined and worked by you. I coach leaders who have been deeply hurt because other people do not understand their assignment. Your assignment is not for others to understand in detail as you do. Your job is not to convince people to validate your assignment. Your job is to influence people to see the value in accomplishing it. Please understand this distinction, and you will save yourself a lot of stress trying to convince people to validate your assignment. When you have a headache, you take pain medicine because your doctor has convinced you that it takes the headache away, and when you've taken it in the past, it did take the headache away. You don't know the mechanism behind the effectiveness of the pain medicine or all the ingredients in it. All you know is that it works. That is how you should view others' assessment of your assignment. Just prove to them that it works for them, that's all. They don't need to understand the details.

Your assignment is external, in the world. Everything about your spiritual, psychological, and physical makeup was customized specifically to enable you to fulfill your assignment. Your purpose is the description of your assignment. Your assignment is the work itself. Your assignment is connected to three Ps: position, people, and place.

Position: The first ones usually have an assignment that puts them in the front of the line. Their position is in the front, the beginning, the alpha. People in this position are usually forerunners, trailblazers, and pioneers; these are people who uncover, invent, and create something that didn't exist. For example, Steve Jobs, the founder of Apple, is considered a forerunner in the technology space. Then we have riders, people who build on what others have done. These are positioned at a time where they ride the coattails of forerunners and build on what forerunners created. Examples are second-generation business owners and artists in older genres that have leveraged on the foundations set by their predecessors. Then we have closers, those who mark the end of an era; these are people positioned at the winding down of a trend.

People: As a leader, your assignment is for a peculiar group of people. This is not discriminatory. Even within ethnicities, race, and other distinguishing characteristics, there is heterogeneity. Your assignment serves a particular population of people. Specifically, people who have the need that your assignment fulfils. You need to know this as a leader that your assignment is not for everyone.

Place: Lastly, your assignment is tied to a particular place. Place is not necessarily a physical location but rather a space, industry, or community. So, your assignment is usually within certain places like the economic place or the media, humanitarian, arts, medicine, business, or religion space.

It is your life's work to continue to uncover layers or versions of your assignment, train for it, and execute it. It will take you all your life to fulfill your life assignment, and that is the definition of a life well spent. This is what brings the utmost fulfillment and satisfaction. This is what people mean when they say, "I want to make a difference. I want to help people. I want to have impact." What they are saying is, "I want to do the work I was assigned to do here on earth. I want to see that work manifest and producing results."

GOALS

Leaders bring their vision to reality and execute their assignment and stay on track with their assignment per time by establishing goals. Leadership is always in service to a particular goal. If you are not achieving your goals or making progress toward them, you are not leading. Goals are posts or markers that let you know your vision is materializing. Goals should not be static or arbitrary. You've probably heard the acronym SMART for goal settings. The acronym says goals need to be Specific, Measurable, Achievable, Realistic, and tied to a Timeline. As a leader, you should have defined markers for each period that indicate success or vision achievement. Organizations craft strategic plans with goals and objectives they define to confirm mission achievement and vision attainment. Accomplishing goals requires a systematic and focused approach. Here is a step-by-step description of how to accomplish goals effectively:

1. **Set Clear and Specific Goals:** Start by setting clear and specific goals. Clearly define what you want to achieve, why it is important, and the timeline for completion. Specific goals provide direction and focus. Your goal must be linked to your vision and be in service to your assignment.

2. **Break Goals into Smaller Tasks:** Divide your main goal into smaller, manageable tasks or milestones. Breaking down the goal makes it less overwhelming and allows you to track progress more effectively.

3. **Prioritize Tasks:** Determine the order in which you need to complete the tasks. Prioritize tasks based on their importance, deadlines, and dependencies. This helps you stay organized and focused on what needs to be done first.

4. **Create a Plan:** Develop a detailed plan outlining the steps you will take to achieve your goal. The plan should include the tasks, deadlines, resources needed, and any potential challenges or risks. I recommend you develop an individual leadership plan that outlines steps for you to build competencies, so you advance as a leader.

5. **Stay Organized:** Use tools like calendars, to-do lists, or project management software to stay organized. Regularly review your progress, and update your plan as needed.

6. **Stay Motivated:** Find ways to stay motivated throughout the journey. Celebrate small achievements, visualize success, and remind yourself of the benefits of accomplishing the goal.

7. **Overcome Obstacles:** Be prepared to face challenges and obstacles along the way. Develop a problem-solving mindset and seek support or advice when needed.

8. **Stay Persistent:** Persistence is key to achieving goals. Stay committed to the process, even when progress is slow, or setbacks occur. Perseverance often leads to success.

9. **Track Progress:** Regularly track your progress against the plan. This helps you identify areas of improvement and make necessary adjustments.

10. **Adapt and Learn:** Be flexible and willing to adapt your approach as you learn from your experiences. Embrace feedback and use it to improve your strategies.

11. **Stay Accountable:** Share your goals with someone else, like a friend, family member, or mentor, who can hold you accountable, provide support, and offer encouragement.

12. **Celebrate Achievements:** When you reach a milestone or achieve a goal, take the time to celebrate your success. Recognize your efforts and the hard work that led to the accomplishment.

Remember that accomplishing goals is a journey, and it's okay to encounter setbacks along the way. Stay committed, stay focused, and believe in your ability to achieve what you set out to do. With determination, planning, and perseverance, you can turn your goals into reality.

We have discussed some tenets you must be intimately acquainted with to lead yourself effectively. Accept your identity, know your capacity, develop your leadership philosophy, draw your vision, work your assignment, and achieve your goals.

PART II

LEADING PEOPLE

5

LEADERS NEED PEOPLE

In a lively village in the heart of Africa, there lived a young woman named 'Amina'. Amina had a dream of creating the most beautiful and vibrant traditional African fabrics the world had ever seen. With a heart full of determination and pride in her African heritage, she set out to accomplish her goal.

Amina spent countless hours at her humble little workshop, diligently weaving and dyeing fabrics, using traditional African techniques passed down through generations. She was convinced her talent alone would make her fabrics stand out and be sought after across the continent and beyond.

As the days went by, Amina proudly displayed her creations at the village market, expecting an overwhelming response. However, to her surprise, the villagers seemed more interested in the fabrics made by the elders in the community, who had been weaving for decades.

Undeterred, Amina decided to work even harder, believing that with sheer determination, she would eventually become the most renowned fabric maker in the village. But try as she might, her fabrics couldn't compete with the artistry of the seasoned weavers.

One sunny afternoon, an elderly woman named 'Mama Ngozi', who was famous for her exquisite beadwork, approached Amina's stall. "My dear, I can see the passion in your eyes and the love in your heart for African fabrics," Mama Ngozi said with a warm smile. "But remember, it takes more than talent to achieve greatness. Sometimes, the wisdom of others can guide us toward success."

Amina was taken aback by Mama Ngozi's words but listened intently as she shared her own journey as a young bead artist. Mama Ngozi explained that she, too, had once been eager to create the most exquisite beadwork, without seeking advice or inspiration from the elders. It was only when she humbled herself and learned from their vast knowledge that her artistry flourished.

Inspired by Mama Ngozi's wisdom, Amina decided to approach the village elders and ask for their guidance. With a newfound sense of humility, she shared her dreams and passion for creating beautiful fabrics that would showcase the richness of African culture.

To her surprise, the elders welcomed her with open arms and hearts. They shared their techniques, stories, and experiences, teaching Amina the intricate art of weaving and dyeing fabrics. They also showed her how to infuse the fabrics with deeper meanings, capturing the essence of African traditions.

As the weeks passed, Amina's fabrics began to take on a new life. The vibrant colors, intricate patterns, and rich symbolism wove a tapestry of African heritage and storytelling. The villagers were captivated by Amina's newfound creations, and her fabrics became highly sought after, not just in the village but across the region.

With the support and wisdom of the elders, Amina's dream had transformed into a reality beyond her imagination. Her fabrics were worn with pride by people from different cultures, celebrating the beauty of Africa and its diverse traditions.

From that day on, Amina became not only a master fabric maker but also a humble student of African artistry. She understood that accomplishing her goal required seeking guidance from the wise and experienced, who held the keys to unlocking the true essence of Africa's creativity and beauty. Amina's success not only uplifted her, but it also brought honor and admiration to her village and its rich cultural heritage, echoing through the heart of Africa for generations to come.

In this story, Amina learnt that as a leader, you need people to accomplish your goals. Alone, she was a fabric maker, but with people, she became an expert in African artistry, the pride of her village, and an exporter of her craft.

A technician does the work; a leader assembles a team that doesn't just do the work but takes up space in the industry. Most people confuse management with leadership. Managers manage events, projects, and things; leaders lead the people who do the work. As the first one, it is common for you to wear the dual hat of management and leadership but know when you are being a manager versus a leader. Leaders cannot scale their efforts without people. In this section of the book, we will dive into the second component of leadership, which is leading people. Mary Kay Ash, the founder of the popular makeup brand, Mary Kay, said, "People are definitely a company's greatest asset. It doesn't make any difference whether the product is cars or cosmetics. A company is only as good as the people it keeps." This is so true because as you can see from Amina's story, it was the team, the elders, and the members of the artistry community in her village that took her from a struggling trade to a successful business. As the first one, once you get a grip on accepting your identity, understanding your capacity, and developing your leadership philosophy, you must be intentional about building an ecosystem to help you drive impact.

When I first started AMA Consulting, within the first year, I hired a part-time assistant; this decision was very instrumental to the growth of the company. I never bought into the mindset of being a one-person business. I strongly believe results are fuller, richer, and more impactful when there is input from a team. Ronald Reagan, fortieth president of the United States, said, "The greatest leader is not necessarily the one who does the greatest things. He is the one that gets the people to do the greatest things."

Leaders who have the mentality of "I alone can solve it" often get torpedoed by risks, threats, and their personal blind spots. Deuteronomy 32:30 says one will chase a thousand and two will put ten thousand to flight. Why is this? It is because of a term called *synergy*. When two individuals or organizations collaborate, their combined efforts often create a synergistic effect, where the whole is greater than the sum of its parts. This means their combined impact is stronger and more significant than what each could achieve separately. This is why leaders build partnerships and encourage people and use social influence to accomplish their mission.

If you study the greatest leaders of our time, they always had a team. As a leader, your team or ecosystem can include a combination of employees, partners, and advisors. These are people who have direct access to you and influence you as a leader. Your team serves the purpose of helping you achieve your goal. You as the leader also use influence to activate, motivate, and empower your team or ecosystem to implement your vision.

Your followers are affected by the work you do, consume your product or service, or have a stake in the work you do. Throughout this chapter, I will refer to your followers or following when I am referring to the broader audience you affect or serve and your team when I'm addressing the ecosystem that implements your vision.

WHO ARE YOUR PEOPLE?

Leadership is about influencing people to harness their talents for use toward achieving a specific goal. The fundamental difference between leaders and managers is that managers manage things, situations, systems, and structures, but leaders lead people. Leaders often must wear both hats, but the primary focus of leaders is to harness the gifts and talents of the greatest resource in the world, which is human beings. This is a popular misconception that inexperienced leaders struggle with. You cannot manage people; you can only influence people.

Influencing is a science and an art. It is a science in the sense that the team/ecosystem must exist to be influenced, so that means you have to identify, recruit, and bring on board a team/ecosystem, and numbers count. Second, your people must have what you need to accomplish your vision. You must have a vision that resonates with the people you want to influence.

Influencing is an art because people are incredibly complex. You cannot override the will of people. You, the leader, are a person too, with the same complexities as the people you lead.

There are 7.8 billion people in the world, and 331.9 million people in the US. People are not a monolith; social categorization is the process through which we group individuals based upon social information. The big three categories are race, sex, and age. Other subcategories include ethnicity, sexual orientation, socioeconomic status, and religion. Further subcategories include family status, culture, generational groupings, professional affiliations, industry affiliation, and civic group affiliations. The way people are socialized makes for a very complex interlacing of numerous factors when leading people.

For example, even in subcategory of religion, most people in a particular religion do not believe the exact same thing and may not resonate with the same appeals. For example, in Islam, there are five main branches or sects; each has its own unique beliefs and customs, but they all have a few beliefs that are common to all. For example, the common beliefs are (1) Tawhid, or belief in the One God, (2) the holiness of the Quran, and (3) the teachings of the Prophet Muhammad. The five major Islamic sects are Sunni, the most popular, Shi'a, the second largest sect, Ahmadiyya, the newest sect, Ibadi, not one of the most popular sects, and Sufism, a unique branch of Islam. These five sects all have different customs, traditions, and practices around gender roles, roles of clergy, and politics. It is therefore erroneous to paint an entire religion with a broad brush and assume that a particular vision will appeal to an entire spectrum of Muslims.

Similarly, when it comes to ethnicity, we see the same dynamic. For example, as a woman of African descent, I find it troubling when people still don't know that Africa is a continent with fifty-four countries. In Nigeria, for example, with 213.4 million people, there are 317 ethnic groups, but most people only know the three major tribes: Ibo, Yoruba, and Hausa. We see again that it is overly simplistic for leaders to target a particular country for followership. People are incredibly diverse; great leaders understand this and do not define people only by social categorization. So how do you know the people you are supposed to influence? How do you identify your followers? You identify your people by getting clear on your vision and why your vision is important. The people who believe in your vision and benefit from it are your followers, regardless of their social categorization. You may notice that a certain age group, ethnicity, or social class resonates more with your vision than others. You may even target that group with your messaging to bring them on board, but always remember, it is the vision that attracts followers. People only follow what benefits them. Your vision must meet a need for the people to follow you. This is the price you must pay as a leader to harness the gifts and talents of your followers or collect the money of your customers or gain the votes of people for office; you must meet a need that is important to them.

My greatest inspiration for a leader is Jesus Christ in the Bible. He is the son of God who was sent to the lost sheep of Israel to give them a new life, free from bondage and oppression. He was the Messiah. The prophecy from scriptures was very clear on who his target audience was and what he was going to do for them. When he came to earth and started his ministry, he showed what this new life looked like. The new life included joy, miracles, signs, and wonders. The deaf heard, the blind saw, people oppressed by demons were set free. He mentioned several times that he was sent to the people of Israel, to his own people; however, remember the complexities of the religious sects I explained earlier? Not all of his people believed in who he was and followed him. In fact, he was killed by the same people he came to save. Even though his people rejected him, he was very focused on them, and his teachings were directed at them. But something shifted in his ministry when people who were not part of his target group wanted to be touched by him. Every sick person wants to be well, regardless of their gender, religious belief, or socioeconomic status. The benefits of his vision and the results he was delivering changed his target audience. It became whosoever will believe. The only criteria for being a Christ follower became to believe in him. This is why Christianity is the largest religion in the world today. If you want followers, produce a solution that will fulfill the needs of the people, and they will follow you.

YOUR PEOPLE NEED WHAT YOU HAVE

As a leader, your people are those who find the outcome of your vision valuable. Your vision must meet the needs of the people who follow you.

Deficiency needs are concerned with basic survival and include physiological needs (such as the need for food, sex, and sleep) and safety needs (such as the need for security and freedom from danger). Behaviors associated with these needs are seen as deficiency motivated, as they are a means to an end.

Deficiency needs arise due to deprivation and are said to motivate people when they are unmet. Also, the motivation to fulfill such needs becomes stronger the longer they are denied. For example, the longer people go without food, the hungrier they become.

Maslow (1943) initially stated that individuals must satisfy lower-level deficit needs before progressing to meet higher-level growth needs. However, he later clarified that satisfaction of a need is not an "all-or-none" phenomenon, admitting that his earlier statements may have given "the false impression that a need must be satisfied 100 percent before the next need emerges" (1987, p. 69).

When a deficit need has been more or less satisfied, it will go away, and our activities become habitually directed toward meeting the next set of needs we have yet to satisfy. These then become our salient needs. However, growth needs continue to be felt and may even become stronger once they have been engaged.

People focus on higher needs after their basic needs have been met. You cannot sell relationship coaching packages to people who have no food to eat or are struggling to keep a roof over their head. Those basic needs must be met before you move to a higher level of need. Leaders must understand the needs of their followers and show them they understand, care about the need, and are making an earnest effort to provide that need within the context of the work.

You can use theories like Maslow's hierarchy of needs and other methodologies to define your core audience as a leader. Who is most likely to see value in what you are trying to do, based on the needs they have? You must be clear on this, especially now, when everybody's an influencer, everybody's trying to get likes and follows; trying to build an audience without understanding the needs of your followers is futile. Understanding the makeup of your following takes time and requires investment of learning. Businesses spend time and money analyzing the behavior of their customers. They study their buying habits, preferences, frequency of purchase, and factors that affect their decision to buy. This analysis helps businesses target their marketing efforts to the people who are most likely to make the decision to purchase the product or service.

Great leaders have to know their audience and their followers. The value of followership is not in quantity alone, but in the likelihood the followers will help fulfill the mission. Leaders must understand the preferences, behavior patterns, preferences, and interests of their followers.

What appeals to the people who follow you? What is it about your goal or mission that excites them? What is important to them? What factors affect their actions? Investing the time to know details about your followers will help you understand them, relate with them, and build influence with them. No matter how great and popular you are as a leader, your message and goal will not appeal to everyone. It is your responsibility as a leader to know why people follow you. This will help you be more effective as a leader. Most emerging leaders do not understand this. The first ones almost always try to reach out to everyone, build for everyone, persuade everyone to follow them but quickly find out through rejection, betrayal, and denials that their capability as a leader is not valuable to everyone.

Understanding your followers makes influencing possible because when you target people who see value in your goal or mission, they already want to be influenced by you. Marshal Goldsmith, an executive coach I admire, talks about how companies need to focus on hiring people who align with their vision and want to be engaged instead of spending millions of dollars creating engagement programs for people who do not want what they're offering. He claims it is not pay, benefits, or work-life balance that makes employees highly engaged and productive in an organization. Employees engage when they believe in the mission of the organization, find meaning in the work, and believe in the organization's values. Great pay, benefits, and work-life balance only enhance engagement, but cannot create it.

Leaders must know what the audience wants to be influenced by them. This can be very difficult for visionary leaders and charismatic leaders who draw a wide audience. They believe everyone should want what they're offering, but not so. Some people may not value what you're offering, no matter how good it seems. Leaders must have humility and wisdom to know who they are really called to lead.

Leadership is the art of influencing people in order to harness their perspectives, ideas, gifts, and talents toward the achievement of a goal. You cannot lead without influencing people. You cannot lead if no one is following you. As a leader, you need people to accomplish your goal, expand your vision, and scale your efforts. You need a team. The first thing Jesus did when he began his ministry was to assemble the twelve, his leadership team. He identified them based on their own skills and interests in alignment with his goal of spreading the word about the kingdom of God. When he called Peter, a fisherman, he said to him, "I will make you a fisher of men." Peter was intrigued by that. He had been catching fish all his life, but here was a great opportunity to catch men, a greater catch. Jesus's vision as the leader aligned with Peter's talent and interests and experience. He didn't need to cajole or control him; he simply influenced him by showing him a greater possibility for his life. People who try to control and cajole people have not mastered understanding of their vision and the interests of their followers. The popular convention is, the art of influencing people is daunting; bringing people together toward a common goal, convincing people to tap into their highest and best self for a particular purpose, is challenging.

It is only daunting if you target people who are not interested in finding out how far they can go in life. If you target such people, you will first have to convince them about the benefits of tapping into their highest self and perform some kind of theatrics to keep them motivated when they have trouble along the way. Jesus didn't have to first explain the concept of fishing to Peter or convince him about the rewards of fishing. Peter already had that interest; Jesus just told him he could fish for something more valuable (the souls of men) and told him the great reward associated with that. If you understand this concept of defining and qualifying your followers, you'll solve half of the issues of being an influential leader.

Even with studying your followers and their preferences and learning their intricacies, influencing can still be challenging because human beings are very complex; people can be difficult to understand in totality. They change. Life experiences can make people change their preferences or alliances. People are multifaceted; people are layered with intricacies that stem from their belief systems, backgrounds, and life experiences. Environmental conditioning can make them respond differently to information and direction from leaders and cause them to change. So as a leader, the art of influencing is continuous, and tactics of influencing may have to be adjusted in a leader/follower relationship.

As a leader, never take people for granted; you must continue to engage your team to find out what is important to them. Don't assume you know. Don't assume because they agreed to follow you, they will always want to be on the ride. You have to know their needs may change; you may have to use a different tactic to motivate and influence them on board the ride. Also, you should know people may decide to stop following you, and that is okay. I have coached leaders who became so attached to a particular person on their team that the entire enterprise nearly collapsed when they left. If you build a team around a set of values instead of individual personalities and strengths, when people leave, you can have continuity of operations.

As human beings, any type of separation hurts. When an employee I had leaned on so much for my business quit somewhat abruptly, my first thought was, *What did I do wrong?* As leaders, we personalize events that occur in our organizations. I later found out it wasn't a matter of what I did but the fact that her needs changed, and at that time, we couldn't give her what she wanted. It wasn't personal. So as the leader, I took time to evaluate her position, the duties she was carrying out, and what we needed as a company. I also realized the company had grown, and we needed a slightly different skillset, so we tweaked the job description and hired a candidate who was a great fit for the role, someone who shared our company values.

I learned a valuable lesson from this experience. This lesson is, you must be very flexible when dealing with people but firm on your values and goals. Yes, change causes some disruption, but that is part of leadership. If you get all bent out of shape every time a member of your team makes a choice different from what you expected, you will lose your focus. Great leaders understand that while you should be intentional with building a team of people who buy into your vision and align with your values, you should also be prepared for contingencies and not take team changes personally.

YOUR PEOPLE GENERALLY SHARE THE SAME VALUES AS YOU

Once people need what you have as a leader, the next way to qualify people through an intake process to see if they are fit to be a part of your team/ecosystem is to test out their values. The most effective way to test for synergy in any relationship is alignment of values. Human beings will always defer to a behavior that operationalizes what they truly believe. No matter how much people pretend or try to adapt to an environment, when they are unguarded, under pressure, or succeeding, they default to behaviors that reflect their values. This is why it can be very costly to engage in significant relationships with people based on what they tell you or how they act in a particular season or circumstance. You really want to scope out what they believe because that will drive how they behave in the long run.

I personally believe that the traditional interviewing process is not very effective in building a team. From my experience, leaders who have very solid teams have had an opportunity to experience team members in various circumstances or have talked to others who have experienced the potential team member in various roles so that they have a realistic characterization of what this person believes. This is why personal referrals and recommendations are still the best way to recruit people to your team or part of your ecosystem.

My youngest sister just landed a consulting position with the World Bank. She was contacted because the office had a need and someone who knew her work and had engagement with her recommended her. She did not apply for a job opening. She shared with me that after the World Bank made her offer, the manager who hired her said to her, "You are everything we were told you are!"

Leaders must learn to be patient and dutiful in checking for value alignment before recruiting team members.

Some organizations now inspect prospective candidate's social media profiles beyond LinkedIn, because their online activity offer an insight to their belief systems. For example, a well-curated LinkedIn profile will be a hard sell for you as a diligent worker, if you are making TikTok videos on different excuses you make for skipping work. Now, the process for checking value alignment is not to judge or condemn anyone but to simply define who is the right fit to be a part of your team. Value alignment does not guarantee a perfect working relationship or absence of conflict.

The most difficult aspect of leadership is leading people. Human beings are inherently flawed, naturally selfish, seeking their own good, seeking opportunities for their own benefits, looking out for their own selves in every situation. However, leaders must understand this about people and still work with the innate greatness and immense creativity in them to achieve a goal. If you, as the leader, are the instrument for leadership, then people are the vehicle by which leadership travels. Now, why do people have to be the vehicle in the age of automation, when we can use technology pretty much for everything, including robots that perform surgeries, medical procedures, and accounting functions? When it comes to leadership, why is it that we need people? Why is it that we need a team? Why do we need to harness the effort of others? Why do we need to leverage the talents, the creativity, the ideas of others? It is for one simple reason: We need people because human beings are simply the most advanced species on earth. Human beings possess resources that are unmatched by technology, resources like empathy and creativity; only human beings can create something that is not of their own kind. Every other living thing reproduces after its kind.

In technology, software is only produced after an algorithm is programmed, but only a human being can figure out what pieces of metal and other materials can make a plane. Only a human being can think up a way to connect to billions of people all around the world through the internet. Human beings create technology. So, this great technology era was birthed by humans, just as the industrial age was. Human beings are the greatest resource.

That is why we need people. Leading people is one of the cornerstones of leadership and the second leg of the three-legged stool of leadership, behind leading self and before leading in an organization.

Some organizations offer development programs to improve their leaders' competencies, with courses on effective communication, conflict management, giving and receiving feedback, emotional intelligence, and so on. These courses are great to help leaders interact well with others, but they often fall short of enabling leaders to understand the role of teams and followers in their leadership journey.

First-time leaders struggle tremendously with the people factor because of the complexities associated with human nature; they are not always well equipped to handle these complexities. Leaders must understand people, as flawed as they are and as complex as they can be. Leaders must know that people carry the hidden treasures for the next great thing, the next thing that will revolutionize the world, the next big thing that will solve the challenging issues we are confronted with.

The next big thing that will open up a new dimension of human experience can only come from people. Leaders who understand this and who know this invest in developing their competencies to lead people. Ronald Reagan said, "The greatest leader is not necessarily the one who does the greatest things. He is the one that gets the people to do the greatest things." I say great leaders are those who set the stage for their people to perform.

Leaders face challenges because they always must execute; they have to be on stage and perform. You can burn out and lose touch because it is simply not possible to make an impact on a large scale on your own. The ego often keeps exceptional leaders from allowing other leaders to emerge, to take the stage; this can be catastrophic if you don't check it. Organizations (and nations) with such leaders eventually crumble because they miss out on the ingenuity of their people. As an executive coach, I have seen a lot of emerging leaders struggle, with senior leaders using their ideas for research papers, policies, and plans but not giving them credit. The hallmark of great leaders is how many great leaders they develop.

Leaders who want to achieve great things on a large scale must find a way to work with people as a leader; there is a saying that if you want to go fast, you go alone, but if you want to go far, you go with a team. No matter how much technology you use to scale your business, you need people. Your software or app is not going to brainstorm a revolutionary idea, convey your mission, highlight your vision, communicate warmly to your customers, solve unpredictable problems, or deal with a crisis. People must do that. This is why you need a team. We humans possess in our minds more solutions to the world's problems than technology could ever come up with.

Everyone is concerned about the takeover of automation and artificial intelligence, ChatGPT, the use of robots in medicine, but remember that ChatGPT cannot tell a story from experience in a way that connects with readers when writing a book; only a writer can do that. The robot cannot respond to an unforeseen crisis based on knowledge of the patient's medical history and experience in the theatre during surgery; only a surgeon can do that. People cannot be replaced. Technology only enhances human experience.

When you understand this as a leader, then it makes sense for you to prioritize putting together a great team, developing the people who are members of your team, investing in them, motivating them, inspiring them, and supporting them. You must see value in people in order to be a great leader; this is the best lens to view the suffering and challenges of dealing with people in leadership. Understanding the value in people helps you look past their shortcomings.

The first ones, let me tell you something you won't learn in an MBA class: Leadership comes with a lot of suffering. This is the terrain; uneasy lies the head that wears the crown. Making decisions and being responsible for them is hard. Putting yourself out there to be the answer to people's questions and needs exposes you to attacks and scrutiny. As a leader, because you're being watched constantly, your flaws are permanently on display. The same people who look up to you because they desperately need someone to believe in and someone to anchor to will turn their back on you once their needs are met. The part of leadership that is glamorized with terms like "boss," "influencer," "CEO," and other prestigious titles is offset by the suffering that comes with the terrain. This suffering is often hidden, unspoken, and unfortunately, rarely addressed, processed, or channeled appropriately. I know this because as a coach, I have had front-row seats to the stories of pioneers, trailblazers, and first-time leaders. Their stories are laced with difficulties and trials. If you have a candid conversation with a leader, you admire and learn of their trials, suffering, and the cost of leadership, you will tamp down your eagerness to be in their shoes.

There's reciprocity for the respect and fame and admiration you get as a leader; there's an equal amount of suffering and pain that comes with it. I will add from my experience in leadership and from the leaders I coach, about 90 percent of the pain and suffering leaders experience comes from people. As a leader, please take this with an open mind. I'm not presenting this information to you from a place of cynicism. The truth is that as a leader, you will experience betrayal; you will experience sabotage.

You will often give more than you receive; that will cause you to carry an appreciation deficit you have to live with. This is the price of leadership, and it often comes from the people you have invested in the most, the people closest to you. The pain and suffering that come from betrayal hurts; people sabotage you, backstab you, call you names, misrepresent you, try to take your position or derail your work. This causes a lot of leaders to adopt the go-it-alone approach. However, that approach does not work for scalability; if you want to reach far and wide as a leader, you need people, flawed as they may be.

The ability to lead people presents leaders with some of their greatest challenges, for two primary reasons. The first reason is, leaders themselves are people and possess the same flaws, the same intricacies, the same complexities as the people they lead. Leaders are not superior in any way, shape, or form to the people they lead. Additionally, leaders cannot create a person. We would all love to be able to create our ideal team member who will match every need within the team and never disagree or make mistakes. An ideal team member will have the exact combination of attributes, skill sets, characteristics, personality, and talents that will be suitable for us to accomplish our goal.

We would love to create a follower who will never push back against us, who will always agree with us, who will perform at the level we want them to perform all the time, but we can't. Not only can we not create another human being, we cannot control another human being. For these two reasons, leading people is difficult, and I want to state that here categorically because few leaders acknowledge the pain and suffering that comes with leading people. I hope in this space, I have been able to name some of the emotions you have struggled with and given voice to the pain of leadership.

These challenges and difficulties affect leaders negatively because leaders are often seen as having something unique in them; people believe that it is easy for them to capture the attention of others and deal with all the issues facing everyone else on the team, but the truth is, leaders are human beings just like their followers. They possess flaws, have their own internal struggles, have challenges, have limitations. Leaders are not immune from the pain of rejection, betrayal, and hurt experienced from team members who fall short in character. Leaders hurt, make mistakes, have character flaws, have been marred by trauma, and have failed many times, and leaders feel. Leaders are human beings.

How then is it possible to influence people when you can't control them, when you as the influencer are also flawed? Leaders must be honest in answering this question for themselves. When I coach government leaders, we answer these questions with honesty, real candor about the impact of these experiences, triggers to their own personal trauma, and assessment of their capacity to endure the pain. Walking this journey, being honest about these questions, plays a big role in your success as a leader. Leaders often start the leadership journey within the family unit. Sometimes, the order of birth thrusts people into leadership; for example, being the first child. The first one all the time in circumstances, family situations that create an opportunity early on in one's childhood, where they have no choice but to take responsibility, I always say people who are great leaders never sought to lead or take responsibility; situations and events demanded it of them, and they answered the call, over and over again, and then they became great leaders.

The person who takes responsibility usually emerges as a leader, the one who steps up, the one who does hard things, the one who makes sacrifices for the benefit of others; they usually rise to the call of leadership, and as such, from their very first experiences, they don't get to choose the people who follow them. The chaos to be organized, problem to be solved, or solution to be created determines the followers. This is a big challenge of leadership. A leader's followers are often interested in the problem the leader is charged with solving. Pastors for example serve as spiritual directors and guides for people who seek faith as a solution to the challenges they face in their lives. People often go to church because they seek wisdom, need healing, want better family relationships, or hope for a financial breakthrough. People we interact with have often experienced brokenness, addiction, illness, a rebellious child, a difficult marriage, financial lack. It is this need that drives them to faith. So as a pastor, you are leading people with problems they expect you to address through your ministry. It should be expected, then, that this terrain may come with challenges, events, and crises that come with behaviors of people in need of a savior. In other words,, it is the problem your followers have that leads them to you. So you as a leader cannot separate your follower from the problem. Every new follower you gain is coming with a problem for you to solve. I chuckle when social media influencers decry the trolls. Why do you think they follow you? They probably follow you because they are lonely, have no real friends and so feel terrible about themselves. Your content solves that problem for them, but the problem that brought them to you will also affect you.

This concept is rarely discussed in leadership programs because it is not popular and not politically correct, but if more emerging leaders knew their followers, customers, congregation, or constituents were very closely related to the problems they are seeking to solve, it would help them manage the expectations of their followers and avoid the betrayal that can happen during the leadership journey.

In organizations like the government, senior executives rarely get to pick their team. Most times, the team is already in place before they assume the position of leadership. Even when you are starting up a new initiative or office, as the leader, you may have little control of the hiring process. There are human resources selection rules and processes that provide candidates for you to interview, and the hiring decision is not totally yours. On occasions in government, for example, political appointees may bring in their own team, but the career government workers who are in that department were usually not hired by them; they didn't pick them, but they have to lead them.

So how do you lead people you didn't create, you cannot control, and you did not pick or select?

In leading people, you must ask yourself this question: Do the people you are responsible for leading want to be led by you? Even if you can't control them and didn't select them, leadership is always more effective when the followers want to be led by their leader. Everyone has the power of choice and free will. To help bring some understanding of how to lead people, I'll offer a model I created to determine and characterize followers you didn't select or recruit. Whenever you lead in a system, in your follower pool, you will have drivers, passengers, and detractors. Drivers are people who align with your leadership philosophy, align with your vision, and act on it. Passengers are those who are indifferent and just come along for the ride. Detractors are people who don't like you as a leader and try to sabotage your efforts.

If you are a leader in any organization, you must know your pool of followers, know the criteria that distinguish drivers, passengers, and detractors for you, and engage people accordingly.

Again, in your follower pool, you should know if this person really wants to follow you and accomplish your mission. That's where you start to define your team makeup. The question doesn't have a definitive answer, like most of the concepts we have discussed in this book; that question has a spectrum of answers because some of the people who follow you, no matter what you do to develop, support, inspire, and motivate them, they will never see anything good in you as a leader. They may very well remain on your team and need to be led by you. There are other people who understand your leadership philosophy, your vision, and they know they are supported, they are inspired, and they are motivated. They will be engaged and will be avid drivers of your goals, so they are not just hearers, they are doers. They take action, bring ideas, manage conflict, and mitigate risks. They move the needle on impact.

There are other people who are in between these two extremes of the spectrum, who are just there for the ride. They do just enough to register their presence and can get off the bus at any time. This is the reality of leadership.

If you sit down with great leaders, they will tell you the ratio of drivers to passengers to detractors generally goes something like 20:60:20, depending on the organization. In politics, for example, it is usually 50:50 on paper, meaning 50 drivers and 50 detractors based on party; however, within the party, you'll see something like the 20:60:20 spread again. Even Jesus had a similar split among the twelve disciples: He had the drivers, Peter, James, and John; they witnessed the transfiguration, were almost always with Jesus, and demonstrated deeper understanding of Jesus's ministry. Judas Iscariot and Thomas the doubter were detractors, whether they intended to be or not, and the remaining seven were passengers, along for the ride; they contributed just enough to be a part of the group.

Everyone thinks you only need drivers to be successful in leadership. Yes, you need a healthy number of drivers to achieve anything as a leader, but passengers and detractors serve a unique purpose too. So, no group is all good or all bad. It is your responsibility to know who is who and use tact in managing the different levels of relationships within your team. Here are some tips:

Drivers: These people are loyal; there is almost no rumor, crisis, or problem that will cause them to leave your side, so appreciate them. One major blind spot leaders have is to become too familiar with their drivers and lose all of their commitment and loyalty. Never take them for granted; continue to support, encourage, and reward them.

Passengers: These are the people who carry out the day-to-day tasks; they are also witnesses. Some underdogs may be in this group, so never underestimate them. Pair them up with drivers, as they may be inspired to improve their performance. Also watch out for those in this group who have allegiance to detractors; they might gang up on you. Educate this group, and show them new things; remember, they are witnesses and spectators.

Detractors: These are the naysayers and the opposition; they run the spectrum of being disagreeable to outright seeking to crash the entire car. These are the people who make you earn your paycheck as a leader. Deal with this group with vigilance and boundaries. These people challenge you to grow as a leader; they can also serve as devil's advocate and save you from danger. They protect you from danger because they force you to be disciplined.

Also, keep people in this group visible; never let them be in the dark within the organization, because they can cause havoc. Have you ever wondered why Jesus put Judas in charge of the treasury, even though he probably knew he had a greedy nature? My theory is, he did that to keep the spotlight on him, to keep him from perpetrating evil until the appointed time. Judas oversaw the money. If any money went missing, everyone knew who was responsible. Visibility forces detractors to at least be accountable. This is why betrayal hurts so much because most detractors are not easily detectable; they prefer to be undercover. When you spot them as a leader, make them visible; it will keep them accountable, at least for a period.

It is your job as a leader to treat everyone in your team equally in terms of provision of opportunity, civility, respect, and support. Your daily encounter with your team members should be based on your leadership philosophy, your ethics, and the policy of your organization. It is also your responsibility to harness the gifts, the talents, the creativity, the ideas of everyone in your team equally; yes, including the ones who don't want to be led by you, if they are willing. Always avail everyone the opportunity to be great within your team but know that some may never take up the opportunity.

Having situational awareness of your team makeup helps you lead effectively; this intelligence should never be used to initiate bias. This is why I recommend every leader has a coach. Discussions about your team makeup and how you navigate among drivers, passengers, and detractors should be with a neutral coach or mentor, not one of your team members. Not even the highest performing driver in your organization should ever hear you vent about another team member. Even if a detractor openly subverts your authority or is rude, vent to a neutral party, and get the ideas and knowledge you need from your executive coach to handle the issue appropriately, even if it means removing the person from the team. I have seen leaders bleed on their team because of legitimate struggles they've had with detractors or even underperforming passengers, and it didn't bode well for them. Always remember that as a leader, you have the most to lose. Again, I will reiterate that every great leader I know has a coach, therapist, and advisor. Coaches help you emphasize behaviors and competencies that make you successful as a leader. Therapists help you process painful emotional and psychological wounds, and advisors/mentors give you tactical suggestions/solutions for your work. I recommend that you get all three. You will need these resources in order to effectively lead people. Because leadership will cause you pain, you need to continue to grow your competency to lead, and you can benefit from others who have more experience than you, like Amina in the story earlier on in the chapter.

Earlier, I mentioned why value alignment is the most significant way to measure synergy, and now, I want to give concrete ways to determine value alignment and show the effect of value alignment and productivity in teams. One of the competencies you need to lead people effectively in your team is the ability to vet people, qualify their capacity, and define their expectations. You need to know if the people you work with align with your leadership philosophy; you should know your team's capacity and their expectations from you. Values are what people believe about themselves, others, and their work. People's values come from their religious beliefs, cultural beliefs, family upbringing, social orientation, and life experiences. Values are entrenched in human beings, whether defined or acknowledged. Whether people have named their values or not, it is the blueprint for their behavior. We all act according to what we believe about ourselves and the situation. This is also true in the workplace. People's competencies will dictate what they can do at work, but their values will determine how they will do it and to what measure.

Leaders are traditionally trained to evaluate competencies in interviews and reviewing resumes, but they may be less skilled in determining people's value sets. Values are also difficult to uncover without close relationships. For example, during the interview process, it is easy to gauge a candidate's competencies through questions and tests, but employers rarely conduct assessments that uncover people's values because the values typically show up in behavior. While scenario questioning gives insight into how people might think about a problem and go about solving it, it really won't tell you how they will act when they face obstacles. In chapter 1, we talked about identity, capacity, values, and how you craft your leadership philosophy. If you continue to practice self-reflection and improve clarity around your own philosophy as a leader, you will train yourself to pick up other people's value systems from their behavior and words. For example, if loyalty is a core value you operate in as a leader, when you see a potential candidate with a resume that shows three places of employment within a one-year period, you may sense this candidate prioritizes other value sets than loyalty and is probably not going to align with your vision and mesh into your organization's culture.

Value alignment is critical for any relationship to function. One of my favorite scriptures is Amos 3:3 (KJV): "Can two walk together unless they are agreed?" This scripture is the yardstick I use to evaluate the viability of any relationship or partnership. In my estimation, value alignment is the critical factor for success in identifying core team members because people's values don't change. When we interview people at AMA, my favorite question to ask is, "What do you believe about the work you applied for?" You can change people's skill level with training, but it is almost impossible to change what they believe.

Everyone has a set of rules they live by, whether informal or formal; everyone has peculiar attitudes to work, to relating with other human beings, and so on. Values are essential in how you live your life, what is important to you. We all have our personal values, whether they are defined or not. Examples are respect, hard work, loyalty, compassion, tolerance, and humility. These are values people believe in and hold dear, and they become the core of who we are. Societies also have specific values; for example, in the US, our values are freedom, liberty, pursuit of happiness, and self-reliance. In Nigeria, my home country, respect is a core societal value. Similarly, organizations have values. These values are usually on the company's website right along with the organization's mission and vision statement. At AMA Consulting, our values are excellence, diligence, integrity, and compassion. Every society has acceptable norms of conduct set by law. This is how we maintain a civil environment. As a leader, ensuring value alignment with you, your organization, and team members is how you set the culture and tone you want for your team and organization. Core team members must agree with your values for you to lead them effectively. They don't need to have the same value set, but they have to agree.

Let me give some more concrete examples. In this era where matters of diversity, equity, inclusion, and accessibility are forefront in organizations, leaders can have fancy statements about providing equal opportunities for all, but if they don't believe all people should have equal opportunities, they will not implement equity policies and monitor them for success. Similarly, you can say you believe in excellence, but if you are a leader who truly believes that checking the box and getting satisfactory marks is sufficient, you're most likely not going to implement corrective actions for improvements or set standards for customer service and work product quality. Leaders often measure the likelihood of performance of their team based on their qualifications, education, and experience. That speaks to capacity; these things tell you they can do the job, but value alignment tells you if they will and to what extent they will go to produce. People who believe strongly about a cause will work day and night in a job they believe is making an impact on what they believe.

Google studied the secrets of effective teams in the organization. This project was called Project Aristotle. It is often said, "The whole is greater than the sum of its parts." The first step of this study was that researchers defined a team. They decided teams are highly interdependent; team members need each other. They plan, decide, work, and share responsibilities of a project. Then they defined "effectiveness." The researchers defined effectiveness in four different ways.

1. Executive evaluation of the team
2. Team leader evaluation of the team
3. Team member evaluation of the team
4. Sales performance against quarterly quota

This comprehensive definition of team effectiveness captures qualitative evaluations, which had a nuanced look at culture and results, and quantitative metrics, such as sales performance, which lacked situational considerations. The researchers conducted reviews of existing survey data, including over 250 items from the annual employee engagement survey and Google's longitudinal study on work and life; they also conducted hundreds of double-blind interviews. Participants were asked questions around items like:

Group dynamics: I feel safe expressing divergent opinions to the team,
Skill sets: I am good at navigating roadblocks and barriers.
Personality traits: I see myself as a reliable worker.
Emotional intelligence: I am not interested in other people's problems.

In summary, the researchers found out how the team worked together benefited the team's effectiveness more than the competencies of each team member.

In order of importance, the major factors that affect team effectiveness at Google were:

1. Psychological safety: Team members feel safe to take risks and be vulnerable.
2. Dependability: Team members get things done on time and meet Google's high bar for excellence
3. Structure and clarity: Team members have clear roles, plans, and goals.
4. Meaning: Work is personally important to team members
5. Impact: team members think their work matters and creates change.

These five factors that affect team effectiveness per this study all pertain to people's beliefs, not their education, experience, or qualification. Creating an environment that is psychologically safe requires leaders and members who believe in respect, tolerance, compassion, and innovation. Teams where there is high dependability can only exist with people who believe in accountability, personal integrity, diligence, and hard work. A team with structure and clarity requires leaders and team members who value order, organization, direct communication, and honesty. You get the point.

When leading people and building a team, value alignment should be a critical consideration for you as a leader, and it starts with you. When you are clear about your values and operate authentically from them, you will quickly attract people who find the same values attractive. The challenge leaders face here is the celebrity culture we have today. Leaders sometime favor people who look like stars on their teams, people who went to the fancy schools, have a particular degree, have name recognition, maybe someone who has work experience with an organization you admire, someone who presents with all the bells and whistles.

All that is great, but if you choose the "shiny stuff" over value alignment, you will have a lot of issues in your team. Does that mean that competency doesn't matter? No, it does not; competence is required to get the job done, so as a leader, you must balance the poles of competence and character when building your team but give character a little more weight because you can build competence, but it is almost impossible for you to change a grown adult's character, and character is based on values.

YOUR PEOPLE ARE THOSE WHO HAVE THE CAPACITY TO GET THE JOB DONE

Knowledge, Skills, Talent, and Ability

In determining your people, I rank value alignment as the single best qualifier for recruiting your team or targeting your followers. After that, I'd say competence is next. Competence is your people's ability to get the job done. Competence includes the following:

Knowledge: Awareness and insight gained by experience or study about a matter, issue, or situation. Knowledge can be gained by exposure to information and experiences, through either formal or informal learning opportunities.

Skills: The appropriate use of ability and knowledge to perform a task. Skill is perfected by practice.

Talent and Ability: Physical, mental, and emotional capacity or power to perform. Ability is linked to our innate makeup and natural predisposition, even though it can be harnessed and cultivated.

Competence is required to accomplish tasks. Leadership is about influencing people to work toward a goal. If you have people who align with your values but lack competence, they will be great followers, but their productivity may be low. The reason I rank value alignment and character higher over competence is because it is easier to build the competence of others rather than their character. Character building is a tedious, slow process that must be initiated and championed by the individual themselves, while competence can be built by mentors, teachers, and experiences. When making a choice to recruit team members, magnificent leaders must balance the polarity of the requirements of character and competence. One cannot function without the other, and both are required for mission/vision accomplishment. Great leaders must have the skill to quickly assess the competence of people they are recruiting for their team across all aspects of competence in relation to the task they want them to perform. This is a critical assessment you must make every time you meet people. I have coached leaders who built their teams with sentiments, hiring family members, friends, or people they like, without properly considering competence. I coached these leaders through difficulty in setting expectations for their team, lack of clarity about roles and job functions of team members, poor reception to feedback and development activities, low productivity, or below standard performance. One or a combination of these issues over time can be disastrous to a project or organization. Even though competence can be built, it requires the enrollment and participation of team members. If you are not clear on the competence level of your team, and you are not candid about expectations and standards, it is difficult to see growth opportunities as opportunities as opposed to punishment.

I'd like to expatiate on all aspects of competence and the role leaders play in developing their people in each aspect.

Jack Welch, former chairman and CEO of General Electric, said, "Before you are a leader, success is all about growing yourself. When you become a leader, success is all about growing others." In order to lead people, you have to develop them. As a leader, you model character and grow competence for your team. How can you grow the competence of your team members? Most first-time leaders do not understand this is a huge component of responsibility and one of the most critical factors of success in leadership. Organizations spend a lot of money on training programs that are not targeted toward specific competencies and so do not provide any significant change in team productivity. While organizational competency models are great, they do not tell the full story of one's likelihood of exceptional performance. Leaders must be skilled in targeting developmental activities to specific aspects of competence. Developing people takes time and intention. We live in a busy culture where calendars are stacked up with meetings from dawn to dusk; also, in this remote/ hybrid work environment, there is limited room for true collaboration between leaders and their teams. Organizations are now experiencing low domain expertise across their enterprise due to Baby Boomers retiring without passing on knowledge to the younger generation.

The onus lies on leaders to be intentional about creating the opportunity to teach as they learn. Establish knowledge sharing-opportunities through collaboration. It will not happen just because you will it. You have to be intentional about it as a leader, or else you'll have a team of people who have worked with you for years but still don't understand the business of the work. At AMA Consulting, we recently launched training webinars where corporate staff share information on our operational and business processes, and billable staff who support our customers share their project highlights. This has increased overall competency of the workforce, as billable staff understand more about our business and corporate staff know the needs of our customers more completely.

KNOWLEDGE

Knowledge is the awareness or insight of new information. Knowledge is illumination; it empowers and helps people make sound decisions and build confidence. Primarily in the workplace, knowledge is assessed by formal education level and work experience. However, as we know, information can become outdated. For example, as a leader, if you are assessing a PhD holder with several years of narrow work experience, their resume may tell you they know theories about their area of domain expertise or program and can perform research and evaluation excellently. Similarly, if you evaluate a master's degree holder's resume, who attends industry conferences, listens to podcasts, reads books, and tracks world events related to their area of expertise, you may discover they know the basis of the theories, can perform the research and evaluation, and more importantly can use the data from research and evaluation to bring about change.

This is the sort of distinction a magnificent leader should be able to make when evaluating the knowledge level of team members. It is beyond the amount of information a person knows; it is whether this person is positioned to consume, digest, and make meaning of changing, new, and relevant information critical to your program success. You need to know how people's knowledge serves the purpose of your goals. Leaders can develop knowledge in their teams by encouraging a culture of continuous learning, creating hubs and avenues for idea exchanges, and setting up communities of practices or centers of excellence around particular topic areas to expand on the body of knowledge of your team.

As a coach who works with teams, I encourage teams to substitute some meetings for knowledge-sharing sessions. The virtual workplace has made this a little challenging; the water cooler conversations devoid of gossip were partly knowledge-sharing sessions, where people shared what they watched on the news, trends, current events, and news from other departments, and used these new findings to solve problems in their teams. These sessions can be created in Microsoft Teams groups and other virtual group settings within an organization.

Additionally, leaders can use a variety of training programs and types, such as instructor-led, on-demand self-paced, gaming, and webinars, to increase knowledge in their teams. Some professions require certifications and continuous learning credits to maintain the certifications; these are all avenues of development of knowledge within a team. As a leader, your responsibility is to make the information available and accessible to all so there is increased knowledge on your team. I coach federal leaders, and one of the challenges new leaders have is information hoarding. Some senior leaders intentionally withhold information from their team to gain leverage. It is counterproductive. As a leader, it is ideal to create best practices for knowledge-sharing; for example, after people attend a conference, they must brief other team members on the highlights and key takeaways; this will dramatically increase the knowledge base of the teams.

As the first one, I want you to know that your knowledge level is your responsibility. Seek information and be proactive about staying up to date with trends because things change rapidly. My father always told me, "You will always be a master over what you know, and the purpose of having knowledge is to give it away." The more knowledgeable your team is, the less problem solving you have to do as a leader.

Experience is defined as contact with and observation of facts or events. People mistake work experience for length of time employed. Some people can be employed in an organization for years and not make contact with facts or events that can increase their knowledge. Additionally, experience can be gained outside the workplace. I have found people with robust life experiences and people who have been exposed to different states, regions, countries outside where they reside are more likely to be open to new things and so make contact with events and facts that make them know more. The higher you go in your career, the more you find out that most of your work involves looking at issues from different angles and coming up with less obvious solutions. Broader and relevant experience makes the knowledge you have rich. As a leader, expose your people to facts and events in their experience working on your team.

SKILLS

Imagine you are a butcher, and knowledge is knowing the right size, shape, and thickness of a fillet; you're skilled in using the right knife, cutting at the right pressure and intensity to get that perfect shape and size. Skill is the application of knowledge. You can only apply what you know, and what you know that is not applied or applied incorrectly will not produce results. Knowledge is acquired through awareness; skill is acquired through practice. As a leader, you must know how to ascertain the skill level of your team for a specific role. For example, managing a project requires these skills: organization, planning, relationship management, scheduling, application of project management methodologies. Skill level depends on duration, scope, and complexity of previous project's management. You gain skill by doing the act of managing projects over and over again, each time doing it better than the first time or to a more complex degree than the first time. You cannot learn skill. You must practice it.

Tony Robbins, a renowned motivational speaker, said that "repetition is the mother of skill." In this era where people are so impatient and not willing to do hard things, it isn't easy to find people with multiple skill levels. As a leader, encourage your team to just do it; don't be so visionary that no one on your team is working on the vision. As a leader, you must create the space for your team to make changes, do hard things, and challenge the status quo. This is how innovation is born. No one created an invention by reading about the subject matter; they experimented and tried repeatedly until they got their Eureka moment. Richard Branson said, "You don't learn to walk by following rules. You learn by doing and falling over."

I have found that our workforce today, while very technologically savvy and emotionally intelligent, is low in skill because we are easily distracted. The older generations stayed in a field for decades and mastered that field. Today, people change professions every few years, depending on the trends. While I think this mindset is great in some regard, it really has not served us well in skill development. Leaders, you must look out for team members who can focus to build their skills; otherwise, you will have quality issues within your organization. Another issue leaders have is that sometimes, when people master a skill after you have taught and mentored them, they leave. This is why again, value alignment is important. As you invest in your team and give them the opportunity to master their skills, ensure that there is value alignment so the skills they develop are in service to the organization too.

I have observed that the first ones, in a bid to not make any mistakes, sometimes fall into the trap of leading their teams with fear instead of leading with courage. As a leader, encourage your team to take chances with new ideas on projects that may not have very high visibility or far-reaching consequences if failure occurs. I always tell leaders you should have a controlled test environment where your team is free to make mistakes and develop skills. In this era of AI and automation, humans are expected to have depth of skill in multiple areas and combine these skills to create magic. If you are a leader and all your team is following SOPs, you are missing out on the ingenuity your team carries. While SOPs are great to set guidelines for how the work should be done, it should not inhibit your team from increasing the complexity of their work. A mentor of mine said the person who gets the big job is the one who outgrew the small one. If you manage a project well, you will one day be able to manage a program (a suite of projects) and eventually manage a portfolio: a suite of multiple programs. You will not be successful in managing a portfolio until you have mastered managing a project.

To build skill, once you have the knowledge or know how to get it, you must be audacious and courageous. Twenty years ago, as a GS 7 in my former employment at the Federal Emergency Management Administration (FEMA), my boss, the division director, asked for a volunteer to coordinate a housing project for our long-term community recovery program. This coordinator would be responsible for arranging meetings with interagency stakeholders for the project. I volunteered because no one else wanted to. It changed the trajectory of my career. Because I had the audacity to raise my hand, I became privy to the information for the program, learnt it quickly, and interfaced constantly with senior government leaders from FEMA and other federal agencies. It was a hard thing I signed up for, but after I mastered it, I never had issues interfacing with senior government executives again.

As a leader, your job is to build that courage in your team and let them know it is okay to be audacious. Never shut down an idea from your team member and say it cannot be done. Even if you know they might fail, let them try and be there to guide and redirect if things go wrong. I remain forever grateful to Curtis Carleton, my boss at FEMA, who allowed me to be audacious. After you try, you must keep trying; after audacity, you need consistency and tenacity to keep trying and improving. If you succeed at one level, increase the complexity, and go to the next level, just like in a video game. If you fail, conduct an honest assessment; gather feedback from your colleagues, leaders, and mentor; make the necessary tweaks and changes; and try again. Keep repeating this process, and you will gain mastery.

Leaders must be masters in their field. As the leader, you should always have valuable input. Never be a hands-off leader because you lack skill. I have coached leaders who got their dream position and allowed the euphoria of success, the title, and the fame to get to their head. They stopped practicing. They stopped sharpening their skills. One day, they became irrelevant in their organization. I believe leaders must maintain a portfolio of work, so they continue to work on their skill. In an episode of *New Amsterdam,* the NBC drama series, there was a severe epidemic outbreak and a shortage of medical personnel. On one scene, the medical director, Dr. Goodwin, threw a stethoscope to Dr. Fulton, the chairman, who was a senior leader at the hospital and told him he had to take on some patients. Dr. Fulton didn't want to do it; he hadn't seen patients in years because he had been a senior executive at the hospital, dealing with donors, government regulations, and the medical board, but Dr. Goodwin reminded him this was his job.

Dr. Goodwin said to him, "You have a medical license, correct? You treated patients for years, correct?"

Dr. Fulton smiled and took the stethoscope and went to the floor in the ER. He was a tremendous value to the younger doctors, who were struggling to bring the epidemic under control. Dr. Goodwin in that moment reminded Dr. Fulton of his skill. We all have something we've been trained for, experienced in, and skilled in doing well. We should lean into that and help our people lean into that as well.

TALENT AND ABILITY

Leonardo da Vinci is often called the most talented man in history, with an IQ of around 200; he was a genius of geniuses in science and art, and never went to school. His famous painting, *The Mona Lisa,* is the most popular painting in the world. Talent and ability simply come from the Creator. Talent and ability can be discovered and cultivated, but they are innate. Shows like *America's Got Talent* and *American Idol* do just that: discover talent. A great leader should be skilled at identifying talent. We all have talents in different areas to varying degrees. A leader should be adept in picking up the gifts and abilities in their team members and channeling them in the right direction. The greatest tennis player of all time, Serena Williams, had coaches throughout her mind-blowing, record-breaking twenty-three Grand Slam wins career, but it was her father, Richard Williams, who discovered her talent. He knew it when he started to train her and her sister. He saw her ability for the sport was above what the average person could do. He said she would be the greatest, and she did.

This is what leaders do. Leaders must suspend pride and respect talent when they see it. Some leaders suffer from an inferiority complex; when they have very talented team members, they become threatened and start to sabotage them. This is not ideal because talent alone cannot get the job done; it must be identified, cultivated, and groomed to blossom. Sport scouts are very skilled at identifying and recruiting talent. They know what to look for, they know where to find talented players and how to bring them on board. As a leader, your team should be confident that you see their talent and ability, and you will make the investment in making it blossom, not only for the benefit of the organization but for the individual's professional and life goals.

RECIPROCITY: WHAT MAKES PEOPLE LOYAL?

In leading people, you must know and apply the principle of reciprocity. In biology, it is called a symbiotic relationship; in physics, it's Newton's law: for every action, there is an equal and opposite reaction. In the Bible, it is the golden rule: Do to others as you want them to do to you. Leadership is an exchange between the leader and follower for mutual benefit. In his book *Start with Why*, Simon Sinek makes the case that people follow and stay committed to leaders because of what's in it for them ultimately. First-time leaders often have experiences of people abandoning ship, leaving mid-project, quitting without notice, going AWOL as soon as something doesn't sit right with them. This happens when leaders don't articulate in their vision what the benefit or reward for following them is (or they articulate it but fail to come through).

This is why I tell leaders, in identifying people for your team, you must make the case for why people should follow you and what their benefit will be. The benefit has to be something that is of value to them, not something you think should be of value to them. If you have identified a great new addition to your team and their values align with that of the work and organization and they have the right skills, knowledge, and talent, your next question should be, what is their expectation, and can I meet that expectation? Leaders always think people should understand them and be willing to stick with them, but followers are people with their own needs, fears, and ambitions too. The minute they feel there is no hope of getting what they need in the relationship, they leave, even if it is for something unknown or unproven to provide better benefit.

Human beings have needs from every relationship. Leaders and hiring managers need to spend more time understanding the needs of potential employees as they do investigating their qualifications. If an employee wants a flexible work-life balance, what does that mean to them? What specific work hours are they looking for? Do they want to be remote fully? Do they want fancy software to do their work? Do they want a family-style work environment? After you find out their needs and expectations, be honest and assess yourself to see if you, as the leader, can meet those expectations. Always remember, there is reciprocity when there is an exchange of equitable value in the eyes of each party in a relationship.

As regards reciprocity, here are some points to consider and questions to ask yourself as you start to lead teams: What do you need to do consistently for the people you lead as a leader? How will you support your people? Can you provide the resources your team needs to perform at the level of your expectation? Can you meet the expectations your team has of you? What is within your sphere of control to provide? Leadership is equipping, correcting, teaching, supporting, motivating, inspiring, and modeling the right behavior for the people you lead. These are your responsibilities to the people you lead; you must let them know what your expectations are. The exchange is that as you let them know what you are asking them to do to help you accomplish your mission, you must tell them why it benefits them to do what you're asking and what the reward will be when they do it.

After you have articulated reciprocity to initiate the relationship, you must execute it with action. Nothing turns a relationship sour like a broken promise. For example, if an employee needs reasonable accommodation due to a disability, and you say you're an equal opportunity employer and they receive that accommodation in the most minimal way, and it was delayed in getting to them, you may have fulfilled the law as an employer, but you have broken a promise they believed you made as part of your brand. Matters like this that are very human in nature often carry more weight than salary and benefits. People want to know you care for them, the person, not just what they can do for your organization.

If you are not able to meet people's expectations, you must be honest and let them know. In the movie *The Greatest Showman*, PT Barnum recruits unique people otherwise ostracized by society to create a show with catchy musical numbers and exotic performers, which becomes the Greatest Show on Earth. However, his ambition drives him to make a bad business decision that cripples the business financially, and his theater burns down. In the scene after the fire, he is sitting in the rubble with his team and basically telling them it's over, the money is gone, the building is gone, and the dream is over.

One of the performers turns to him and says, "We're not going to allow you to quit. This was not just a job for us. You showed us off when our own mothers were ashamed of us; you gave us a family."

Here, you see the power of reciprocity. Beyond a job, PT Barnum gave these misfits public value that had never been assigned to them and put them in a tribe so they each felt less weird. He told them, "People from all over the world are going to come to see you." And he kept that promise. In exchange for the esteem he gave them, they gave him loyalty and support, even when disaster struck. Leaders often underestimate the power of reciprocity and its connection to influence and loyalty.

I always say when you see someone people follow relentlessly, whether they are wrong or right, it is because they are meeting a psychological need of the followers that supersedes a material need; people will follow someone who knows how to speak to that psychological need even when that person acts against their interest materially. This is why some leaders can manipulate people and turn them into cults.

Always have a pulse on what is important to your team and why it is important to them. Sometimes, if they have gaps in their skill sets and want to learn, you can provide the training, tools, resources, coaching, and involvement they need to be able to function in the capacity you want them to. Other times, it is just about being supportive, asking the simple question: Are you okay? Leadership is not just about bossing people around and telling them what to do. It's also about being there to help when people get stuck, when they are confused, when they're demoralized; when they need help, you must be there to support them. You cannot be aloof. It is your responsibility to make your people feel supported, to the best of your ability. It is also your job to inspire the people you lead because doing great things is hard; if you are going to ask people to sacrifice and come on board with your goal, weather the storm with you during crises, when things are hard, you have to inspire them. You must give them a reason to have hope. You should feed their joy; not be the source of their joy but feed their joy.

The law of reciprocity is very powerful and not studied enough in leadership. Oftentimes, leaders are so visionary that they miss the small things their teams are asking for. Mindfulness helps a lot with providing reciprocity. For example, making a phone call to an employee who was hospitalized to offer comfort, human being to human being, can create an indelible memory of "You were there for me when I was down" in that employee's mind. Mindfulness helps you notice the moments and opportunities to give back to those who give so much to you as a leader.

Also, when it comes to reciprocity, honesty is the best policy; never overpromise and underdeliver. Be candid about your capacity as a leader to your team. This is why your leadership philosophy is important because you can set the expectations upfront. Do not be afraid to say "no" to someone who wants what you cannot give. Reciprocity is not a license to turn into a people pleaser. If you have to twist yourself into a pretzel to get your team to perform and be engaged, they are not supposed to be with you. It is not sustainable. As a leader, you cannot get your sense of worth from your team. If you need their constant praise and approval to feel worthy, you will cultivate a dependent relationship that will be counterproductive to your success. Let the reciprocity be organic, fitting, and authentic.

6

RELATIONSHIP MANAGEMENT

So far, we have discussed how leaders should engage with people, primarily how they should engage with their team, people who help them achieve their mission by doing the work and their followers, people who are affected by their work. Leadership is facilitated by relationships. As a leader, your relational capacity is directly proportional to your social influence. The better you're able to define, cultivate, nurture, and qualify your relationships (and sometimes severe them), the more influence you'll have over people in your sphere. Relationship management is one of the components of emotional intelligence. Relationship management includes properly defining the purpose, nature, and structure of a relationship; being intentional about cultivating the relationship through various seasons, having the wisdom and tact to adapt and change as the relationship evolves; and severing the relationship, if need be.

The key ingredients for relationship management are empathy and understanding. I always say leadership is people business. I always say that as a leader, I am in the people business. A leader must believe every human being is whole, resourceful, and worthy of respect; people deserve what they need and are willing to work for. I know this seems basic, but some people don't believe that all people are worthy of respect and being valued. Some people believe those who are not like them or who don't agree with them have no value. A leader must suspend judgment and bias when attempting to connect with people and first see them as human beings with God-given rights and earned privileges.

If you are a leader who sees people from the perspective of their function or role in your agenda, you will not have sustainable relationships, period. People can tell when you really care about them as a person or when you only care about what they do. This is what empathy is, caring for the whole person, and you care by going close. You must demonstrate a willingness and interest in getting close to the people you intend to be in a relationship with as you lead. Empathy requires an investment of openness and moving in. Moving in looks like asking people how they feel about an idea, what their thoughts are, why they execute actions a certain way; openness looks like suspending all judgment and taking their response for what it is and not what you think it is. You cannot have empathy for someone you don't know, you cannot know a person if you are not close to them and interested in what makes them who they are, and you cannot understand them if you are not open.

In order to understand people, you need to respect them enough to believe what they tell you about themselves, in their words and deeds. We often come into relationships with biases and preconceived notions of the other party, based on their role or function in the relationship. Relationships are built between two people, two human beings, not two titles, not two job descriptions, not two roles or two functions. When you have empathy for and understanding of a person, then you can manage a relationship with them well.

In leading people, it is critical to develop the skill of relationship management because it will well help you

- build trust and credibility with people so your words and directives have weight and mean something to them,
- communicate effectively with people so they know your expectations,
- empower, motivate, and inspire your team so they stay on board and on course with your mission, and
- manage crisis and conflict when they come up.

BUILDING TRUST

George MacDonald, the Scottish author and poet, said, "To be trusted is a greater compliment than being loved." And I believe this completely. Leaders often underestimate the power of trust. Trust is an instrument of leverage. When people believe you are on their side, you'll act in their best interest, and you have their back when they need you, you can pretty much get them to do anything for you. Stephen R. Covey, American educator and author, said, "Trust is the highest form of human motivation. It brings out the very best in people."

One of the prominent psychological theories related to trust is the Social Exchange Theory. Proposed by Thibaut and Kelley in 1959, the Social Exchange Theory says that people's behavior in social relationships is based on the perception of rewards, costs, and the comparison level for alternatives.

According to this theory, people do a cost-benefit analysis of their interactions with others. They evaluate the potential rewards they can receive from a relationship, such as emotional support, companionship, or material gains, and the likelihood they will receive the rewards, and compare it to the costs involved or what they are required to do, such as time, effort, and emotional investments. If the likelihood of receiving that reward is low, they naturally will not be willing to expend the costs you're asking them for. Trust plays a critical role in the Social Exchange Theory. As people engage in ongoing interactions, they develop a level of trust based on the consistency and reliability of the other person's actions. Trust strengthens the commitment to the relationship and influences the willingness to continue investing in it. Therefore, trust gives leverage to the one who is trusted over the one who trusts. This is why when trust is broken, it creates such a huge emotional and psychological wound.

If trust provides leverage and gives power, then it must be carefully guarded and not abused. To build and maintain trust as a leader, generally you must do three things consistently:

1. Keep your word.
2. Be who you say you are.
3. Be honest, even if it requires exposing your flaws.

These things seem very easy to do but can become challenging to adhere to consistently, depending on the stakes in the situation. We are in a time of heightened personal ambition, competition, and fast successes. The internet and social media put people under pressure to be successful, rich, and influential. Everywhere you turn, there is a program that can make you successful in ninety days. Building trust is not a microwavable event. Building trust with people is a gradual process that requires consistency, empathy, and open communication. Here are some tips to keep your word, be who you say you are, and be honest:

1. **Be Reliable and Consistent:** Demonstrate reliability by following through on your commitments and promises. Consistency in your actions and words helps establish a sense of dependability and builds confidence in your character.

2. **Communicate Openly and Honestly:** Practice open and honest communication. Be transparent about your intentions, feelings, and expectations. Avoid deception or withholding crucial information, as it can erode trust quickly.

3. **Act with Integrity:** Uphold strong moral principles and ethics in all your interactions. Adhere to your values, even in challenging situations, to show you can be trusted to make ethical decisions.

4. **Listen Actively:** Show genuine interest in others by actively listening to their concerns, ideas, and opinions. Pay attention to their needs, and validate their feelings, fostering a sense of being heard and understood.

5. **Be Empathetic and Respectful:** Empathy and respect are essential for building trust. Try to understand others' perspectives, experiences, and emotions. Treat everyone with respect, regardless of their status or background.

6. **Keep Confidential Information Secure:** If someone shares sensitive or confidential information with you, honor their trust by keeping it secure and not sharing it with others without permission.

7. **Apologize and Take Responsibility:** If you make a mistake or unintentionally break trust, take responsibility for your actions, and offer a sincere apology. Acknowledging your errors shows humility and a commitment to improving.

8. **Avoid Gossip and Negative Talk:** Engaging in gossip or speaking negatively about others can harm trust. Focus on positive conversations and avoid participating in conversations that undermine trust between people.

9. **Demonstrate Competence:** Showcase your skills and expertise in your area of work or interest. When others see your competence, they are more likely to trust your abilities and judgment.

10. **Be Patient:** Building trust takes time, and it can't be rushed. Be patient and consistent in your efforts, allowing trust to develop naturally over time.

11. **Be Supportive and Encouraging:** Offer support and encouragement to others in their endeavors. Celebrate their successes, and help them during challenging times, showing you are invested in their well-being and growth.

12. **Avoid Overpromising:** Be realistic about what you can deliver. Avoid making promises you can't keep, as it can lead to disappointment and erode trust.

If you do these things, you will have trusting relationships and build leverage to be used in service of good and not for harm.

DEFINING AND CATEGORIZING RELATIONSHIPS

As part of relationship management, you must be skilled in defining relationships appropriately and managing each relationship appropriately. This clear definition and unique management of sections or core groups of relationships establishes boundaries that keep you, the other party, and the relationship safe. Generally, as a leader, your relationships will fall into one of the following categories: team member, colleague, acquaintance, public follower, stakeholder, and partner.

TEAM MEMBERS

As a leader, your team is a vital asset that plays a significant role in the success of your organization. These are individuals who work closely with you, report directly to you, and have firsthand knowledge of your vision, goals, and assignments. They are the ones responsible for executing your strategies and helping you achieve your mission. Therefore, it is crucial for you to select your team carefully.

In the Bible, we see the example of Jesus, who, at the beginning of his ministry, chose twelve disciples to be part of his close-knit team. His decision was intentional and purposeful because he knew his team would be instrumental in spreading his teachings and carrying out his mission. Similarly, as a leader, you should take an active role in selecting your team because they will be instrumental in achieving your vision and goals.

Here are some reasons why you should pick your direct reports:

1. **Shared Purpose and Common Goals:** A well-functioning team should have a shared purpose and common goals. As a leader, you have a specific vision in mind, and you need team members who are aligned with that vision. By selecting your team, you can ensure everyone is on the same page and working toward a unified objective.

2. **Complementary Skills and Expertise:** Effective teams consist of individuals with diverse skills and expertise that complement each other. As a leader, you know the specific talents and competencies required for your team to succeed. By personally selecting team members, you can ensure you have the right mix of skills to tackle various challenges.

3. **Trust and Comfort:** Leading a team requires a strong sense of trust and comfort among team members. When you handpick your team, you are more likely to choose individuals you can trust and feel comfortable with. This foundation of trust fosters open communication, collaboration, and a positive work environment.

4. **Emotional Involvement and Reciprocity:** Effective leadership involves emotional involvement with your team members. When you personally choose your team, you are more invested in their success and well-being, which fosters a sense of reciprocity and mutual support.

5. **Cultural Fit:** Your team should also align with the organization's culture and values. As a leader, you understand the culture best

and can select team members who will thrive in that environment, leading to higher team cohesion and productivity.

6. **Accountability and Responsibility:** When you are involved in selecting your team, it reinforces accountability. Team members know they were chosen for a reason and have a responsibility to contribute to the team's success.

7. **Empowerment and Motivation:** When team members are handpicked by you, they feel a sense of empowerment and motivation. Being chosen for a specific role by you can boost their confidence and commitment to their tasks.

While you play a decisive role in selecting your team, it is essential to ensure transparency and fairness throughout the process. Encouraging feedback and input from team members during the selection process can further enhance team buy-in and commitment.

In conclusion, as a leader, you should actively take part in selecting your team, as they are instrumental in achieving your vision and goals. By handpicking your team members, you ensure a shared purpose, complementary skills, trust, and emotional involvement, leading to a cohesive and high-performing team that works collaboratively to achieve objectives.

PARTNERS

Partnerships imply a relationship where individuals or entities come together to work jointly on a project, venture, or endeavor. This type of relationship involves sharing responsibilities, resources, and accountability. Let's further expand on the concept: As a leader, this is the most challenging relationship to find and cultivate because it requires sharing risk and reward. The nuances involved in calculating the value of the risk and reward of each partner can be challenging to navigate. This is why most people go it alone when they launch a venture or start a new project.

Collaboration forms a key aspect of a partnership, as partners work together and combine their knowledge, skills, and expertise to achieve a common goal. Different perspectives are brought to the table, enhancing problem-solving and decision-making processes. Partnerships are built on a shared vision or set of goals. Both parties have a clear understanding of what they aim to achieve together, and they align their efforts toward the same objective. A healthy partnership benefits all parties involved. But due to human complexities, it can be difficult to get perfect equity in benefit sharing in partnership. Whether it's increased revenue, improved efficiency, expanded market reach, or other advantages, both partners gain value from their joint efforts.

Partners often pool their resources together for increased impact, which may include financial investments, expertise, technology, or human capital. This allows them to leverage each other's strengths and maximize their collective capabilities. Risk-sharing is an essential aspect of partnership. When embarking on a joint venture or project, partners share both the potential rewards and risks associated with the endeavor. Spreading the risk ensures no single party bears the full burden of adverse outcomes. This aspect of a partnership is very appealing to leaders, but emerging leaders must be very clear on what they need out of the partnership. Everything we discussed in part I of this book regarding leading yourself will serve you well in establishing partnerships.

Successful partnerships are built on trust and transparency. Open communication, honesty, and a willingness to address concerns foster a strong and sustainable partnership. Partnerships are most effective when each party has defined roles and responsibilities. This minimizes confusion and ensures that everyone knows their contribution to the shared objective. Partners must be committed to the partnership's success while also being adaptable and flexible to address changing circumstances or evolving project requirements. Like any collaborative effort, partnerships may encounter disagreements or conflicts. Effective partners approach these challenges constructively and work together to resolve them.

Many partnerships are formed with a long-term perspective, aiming for continued growth and success beyond the initial project. As such, it's crucial to nurture the relationship and maintain open communication.

Overall, partnerships provide a powerful mechanism for achieving shared objectives by combining resources, expertise, and effort. Establishing partnerships on a foundation of trust, mutual benefit, and risk-sharing can lead to successful and sustainable outcomes for all parties involved.

At AMA Consulting, we would not have grown to the size we are now without trusted partners. Government contracts often require skills that a small business like ours does not possess in totality. When we work with partners, we start with value alignment because that is the only way we can work together in service of the customer. We check for Complementary qualifications to ensure that we can complement each other and not compete against each other; we audit capacity of both firms to meet the requirement of the contract and use open communication. We have worked with some larger companies for over five years, and these partnerships are mutually beneficial. We are only able to accomplish this because I train my leaders to know the importance of relationships and to learn how to manage them.

COLLEAGUES

As a leader, you will find your colleagues are other leaders in similar roles as you. Look for them within the same organization, or if you are a CEO, they may be in the same industry. These colleagues will play various roles in your leadership journey, serving as advisors, accountability partners, or supporters.

Recognize the value of building relationships with senior colleagues who can act as mentors, providing guidance and insights based on their experience and expertise. Their mentorship will help you navigate challenges, make informed decisions, and grow as a leader. On the other hand, understand the significance of mentoring junior colleagues, sharing your knowledge, and empowering them to reach their full potential.

While forming these connections, be mindful that some colleagues may be competitors in certain contexts. In such cases, be careful in establishing clear parameters around the relationships to maintain professionalism and protect the interests of your organization.

Having colleagues as advisors and accountability partners is essential for you to gain diverse perspectives and receive constructive feedback on your leadership decisions. These interactions will allow you to broaden your horizons, identify blind spots, and refine your strategies.

Moreover, the support and encouragement from your colleagues will be invaluable. Sharing successes and challenges with like-minded leaders will foster a sense of camaraderie and create a support system that keeps you motivated during both triumphant and difficult times.

Believe that a strong network of colleagues will help you stay updated with industry trends, best practices, and innovative ideas. Regular interactions and knowledge-sharing with colleagues will enable you to stay ahead in your leadership role and drive positive change within your organization.

Your colleagues as fellow leaders will play crucial roles in your leadership journey. They will provide valuable mentorship, act as advisors and accountability partners, and offer unwavering support. Be mindful of the various roles colleagues can play, and actively seek to build meaningful relationships that contribute to your growth as a leader and the success of your organization.

ACQUAINTANCES

An acquaintance is a person you are familiar with or have met, but there's no close or intimate relationship. Acquaintances are individuals you know to some degree, within the context of your work. They may be people you have met through social events or conferences; you might have some basic knowledge about them, but your interactions with acquaintances are generally limited compared to those with close relationships.

Acquaintances can be friendly and amicable, but they typically do not share a deep emotional bond or a significant level of trust. Interactions with acquaintances may be occasional and centered around specific situations or shared interests.

It is essential to differentiate between acquaintances and close relationships with your team or colleagues, as the level of intimacy and personal connection differ significantly. While acquaintances can be valuable in various social and professional settings, understand they have no commitment to your success and do not owe you any reciprocity because there has not been a demand placed on the relationship. I have seen many emerging leaders get carried away and mischaracterize acquaintances based on a one-off comment or occasional kind gesture and get burnt when they place high expectations on them. I have experienced that myself.

I have found, though, that acquaintances can be great connectors, information hubs, and potential referral sources. One practice I have is when considering a team partner for my business, I contact a few acquaintances to see if they have any "word on the street" about that company. If they can provide any information, that will confirm what they say about their values.

STAKEHOLDERS

In your role as a leader, it's essential to recognize the work you do, your actions, and your words have a significant impact on stakeholders. As the first one, quickly learn that your impact is broader as you go higher in leadership. I have coached leaders who committed unforced errors simply because they underestimated the reach of their influence. With more influence comes more responsibility. These stakeholders encompass various groups, each with its unique interests and expectations. Let's delve into who they are and how they are influenced by your leadership:

Your Team: Your team members are among the most crucial stakeholders. They directly work with you, reporting to you and relying on your guidance and direction. Your leadership style, communication, and support profoundly affect their morale, productivity, and job satisfaction. As a leader, you have the responsibility to foster a positive and motivating work environment that nurtures their growth and empowers them to excel in their roles.

Colleagues and Other Employees: Besides your immediate team, you have colleagues and employees in other departments or divisions within your organization. Your decisions and actions can ripple throughout the organization, affecting other teams and individuals. Collaborating effectively with colleagues and maintaining positive relationships foster a culture of teamwork and mutual support, benefiting the entire organization.

Decision Makers: Decision makers around your work, such as senior executives, board members, or stakeholders from other departments, are crucial. Your work and performance directly influence their perspectives and assessments of your team's contributions to the organization. Engaging with decision makers, demonstrating the impact of your team's efforts, and aligning your goals with the organization's vision are essential for building trust and credibility.

Customers: Customers are among the most critical external stakeholders. The products or services your team provides directly affect their experiences and satisfaction. As a leader, understanding customer needs and expectations is vital in guiding your team to deliver value and maintain strong relationships with clients. Happy customers lead to business growth and a positive reputation in the market.

In managing relationship with stakeholders, keep these tips in mind:

Active Communication: Engaging in open and transparent communication with all stakeholders fosters a shared understanding of goals and expectations. People are craving content more than ever. The quickest way to erode trust is to be a silent leader. People want to hear from you often. They want your thoughts; it helps boost their confidence in you. Regular updates, listening to feedback, and addressing concerns build trust and foster a sense of inclusivity. Sending quarterly reports to the board will not suffice; you must engage and tell stories around the numbers, performance, and milestones your team is achieving.

Empathy and Understanding: Understanding the needs and perspectives of different stakeholders enables you to make decisions that balance their interests. Empathizing with your team's challenges and customers' preferences helps you lead with compassion and make informed choices. Balancing interests is a skill in relationship management when you are in a relationship with two parties with opposing interests. For example, senior leadership targets with resource limitation of your direct report. These nuances with stakeholders must be balanced with understanding and empathy.

Strategic Decision-Making: In managing relationships with various stakeholders, your decision-making must be strategic. Consider the implications on various stakeholders, the goals and mission, and the organization as a whole. Weighing the short-term and long-term impact helps you make choices that align with the broader objectives.

Intentionality: Be intentional in building strong relationships with stakeholders. It creates a supportive network and enhances collaboration.

I always say you want to build allies, champions of your work. Position yourself in the minds of people. Do you want to be known as the go-to person for ideas, the connector, the course corrector? Be intentional when nurturing relationships with stakeholders. Nurturing relationships with colleagues, decision makers, and customers fosters a sense of partnership and mutual growth. Remember that your leadership has a broader impact beyond your immediate team. Understanding and actively engaging with stakeholders contributes to the success of your organization, its reputation, and the fulfillment of your shared goals. As you lead, keep the interests of all stakeholders in mind, striving to create a positive and lasting impact through your work.

PUBLIC FOLLOWERS

Public followers are individuals who publicly follow you or subscribe to your organization on social media platforms or other online channels. These followers actively choose to connect with and receive updates from you, often expressing their support, interest, or admiration for your content, activities, or messages.

Public followers include your fans, customers, supporters, and those who share similar interests with the public figure or organization. They engage with the content shared by the account they follow, which can include posts, videos, articles, announcements, or any other form of online communication. Leaders have gotten into the habit of making decisions to increase public following in this social media era. I understand that followership on social media channels denotes influence and can translate to revenue, but as a leader, you must manage the relationship with public followers in a way that is authentic for you.

The term "public" signifies the social media account or online presence of the person or organization is accessible and visible to a broad audience. It is not limited to a private or exclusive group, and anyone interested can follow or view the content. Again, this increased exposure carries increased risk. The higher number of public followers you have, the more hate, condemnation, comparison, and scrutiny you're exposed to as a leader.

Public followers play a crucial role in amplifying your reach and influence; we have all heard of people who have become famous from a video that went viral. Their engagement, likes, comments, and shares contribute to increasing the account's visibility and building a community around the content shared. The key is to always point your public followers to your assignment, vision, and goals. Don't have a following just for the sake of fulfilling the need to be loved and admired. Remember, a leader is one who knows the way, goes the way, and shows the way. When you amass a following, make sure you're showing them the way you're going.

TERMINATING/CHANGING RELATIONSHIPS

As an emerging leader, you must be skilled in terminating or recategorizing relationships. We are socialized to see the end of a relationship as a loss or the change of a relationship as a negative thing. As human beings, we form attachment to ideals and ideas, and make up stories about our experiences to cope and survive. As a leader, you may have team members, partners, colleagues, or stakeholders with whom you've cultivated a good relationship. You were intentional and used all your skills of relationship management: empathy, understanding, rapport. You worked hard to ensure reciprocity in that relationship, and then things went sour. The relationship stopped being beneficial to you, stopped yielding benefits, or became outrightly harmful. For fear of losing that connection, we form an unhealthy bond to the idea or ideal of that relationship, even though in reality, that ideal does not exist. This can be detrimental to your welfare as a leader and can negatively affect your other relationships, stall your progress, and in some extreme cases, stop you from doing your assignment.

AVOIDING TOXIC RELATIONSHIPS

Once upon a time, there was a driven and ambitious woman named 'Emma', who had a brilliant business idea. Eager to turn her dreams into reality, she knew she needed a partner who could bring complementary skills to the table. That's when she met John, a charismatic and successful businessman with experience in marketing and finance. Impressed by his credentials, Emma thought she had found the perfect partner to help her business flourish.

At the beginning of their partnership, everything seemed promising. Emma and John worked well together, combining their expertise to build a successful venture. The business started to gain traction, and they were making progress toward their goals. However, as time went on, Emma began to notice subtle changes in John's behavior.

He became increasingly domineering and dismissive of Emma's ideas, often taking credit for her contributions. Emma tried to reason with him, hoping that their initial synergy would return, but John's toxic behavior only worsened. He started undermining her decisions, making unilateral choices without consulting her, and even belittling her in front of others.

Fearful of losing the progress they had made, Emma hesitated to sever the partnership. She worried about the potential repercussions and the impact it could have on the business. But as the toxic dynamic escalated, Emma began to see the toll it was taking on her well-being and the business's performance.

The turning point came when a major deal fell through due to John's reckless decision-making. The business was now in jeopardy, and Emma knew she had to take action. Summoning her courage, she decided enough was enough.

In a private meeting, Emma calmly but firmly expressed her concerns and informed John she could no longer continue with the partnership. She spoke with conviction, asserting her worth and the value she brought to the business. While John tried to manipulate her emotions and guilt-trip her into staying, Emma remained resolute in her decision.

Severing the toxic partnership was not an easy process, but Emma knew it was the only way to preserve the business and protect her vision. As she untangled herself from the toxic relationship, she found a renewed sense of empowerment and independence.

With a clear mind and newfound freedom, Emma dedicated herself to restructuring the business and surrounding herself with a supportive team. She sought out mentors and advisors who recognized her potential and appreciated her contributions.

As time passed, the business began to thrive once again. Emma's determination and courage in ending the toxic partnership paid off. She learned a valuable lesson about the importance of self-worth and the impact toxic relationships can have on both personal and professional life.

In the end, Emma emerged as a stronger, wiser, and more resilient entrepreneur. She turned her business into a roaring success, proving that sometimes, summoning the courage to let go of toxic relationships is the key to unlocking one's true potential and achieving greatness.

Just like death is a part of life, ending relationships is a part of relationship management. You are not a bad person when someone leaves your organization, when you leave a group, or when you cut ties with a partner. Change in relationships is inevitable; it is part of the journey. I deliberately discussed relationship management and qualifying relationships in depth because it is the best defense against having to severe relationships in a nasty way. We've all seen music groups break up. Some groups like Destiny's Child had each member go on to pursue solo careers while remaining friends, while other groups had nasty breakups, like the Spice Girls, the groundbreaking girl group that dominated pop music in the late 1990s. In 1998, Geri Halliwell, also known as Ginger Spice, left the group, citing differences with her bandmates. The abrupt departure of one of the group's key members led to the eventual disbandment of the Spice Girls. The Fugees were a hip-hop group featuring Lauryn Hill, Wyclef Jean, and Pras Michel; they achieved tremendous success in the mid-'90s with their album, *The Score.* However, internal tensions and conflicts between the members eventually led to the group's breakup in 1997.

Various factors can cause a relationship to reach its end, such as abuse, toxic behavior, low performance, unmet expectations, vast difference in values, lack of trust, and lack of reciprocity. As individuals, we have a threshold of how long we want to manage conflicts before we decide the relationship no longer serves its purpose. This is why your leadership philosophy is important. As a leader, you must be true to your values. I say if a relationship repeatedly violates the core of your value set and does not serve its purpose, you need to evaluate it objectively. Look at the cost-benefit of repurposing or redefining that relationship. See if there's a way to recategorize that relationship so you can still leverage the synergy that was built. However, if a relationship violates your core values, feels toxic, is harmful to your well-being or your team's, or threatens to abort your mission, then it is time to honorably terminate it.

Use this yardstick when you have to remove people from your team, severe a partnership, or recategorize relationships with colleagues or stakeholders. As CEO and an employer, I have discovered that whenever

I had to let someone go from the organization or whenever someone quit, it was because their values and needs were not aligned with the work, and they were not honest about it (or their needs changed midway). People are always excited about the benefits of taking on an exciting role but often neglect to account for the demands this new role will bring. The truth is, sometimes we take on roles but don't know what it will take to be a top performer in that role; other times, events occur that may affect our capacity level. Sometimes, people change and want something different. So this aspect of leading people is inevitable. Someone once said, "Endings are just opportunities for new beginnings."

Ending a professional relationship amicably is essential to maintain a positive reputation and avoid burning bridges. Whether it's with a colleague, business partner, or employee, here are some tips to handle the situation respectfully and professionally:

1. **Plan the Conversation:** Before initiating the conversation, take some time to plan what you want to say and how you will deliver the message. Be clear and concise about your decision, avoiding unnecessary details or blame.

2. **Choose the Right Setting:** Pick a private and neutral location for the conversation. If an in-person meeting is not possible, a phone call or videoconference would be more personal than an email.

3. **Be Honest and Direct:** Be honest about your reasons for ending the professional relationship, but avoid being confrontational or blaming. Stick to the facts and focus on the decision itself rather than personal attacks.

4. **Avoid Negative Language:** Use neutral and positive language during the conversation. Refrain from using negative or harsh words that may escalate tensions or hurt feelings.

5. **Express Gratitude:** If the professional relationship has had positive aspects or achievements, express gratitude for the opportunities and experiences you have shared.

6. **Offer an Explanation (If Necessary):** If the other person asks for an explanation, be prepared to provide a clear and concise reason for your decision. However, you are not obligated to disclose more than you are comfortable sharing.

7. **Listen Actively:** Give the other person an opportunity to express her or his feelings or thoughts about the situation. Actively listen without interrupting, even if it becomes emotional.

8. **Stay Professional:** Maintain a professional and calm demeanor throughout the conversation. Avoid getting emotional or defensive, as it can lead to a more challenging exchange.

9. **Discuss Transition Plans:** If necessary, discuss a plan for transitioning responsibilities or projects to minimize disruption and ensure a smooth handover.

10. **Follow Up in Writing:** After the conversation, follow up with a brief and polite email to confirm the discussion and any agreed-upon action steps.

11. **Maintain Respect and Politeness:** Even if you no longer have a professional relationship, treat the other person with respect and politeness in any future encounters or interactions.

12. **Don't Burn Bridges:** Ending a professional relationship amicably allows for the possibility of future collaborations or references. Avoid burning bridges by maintaining a positive attitude and leaving the door open for potential reconnections.

13. **Take the Lessons Learned:** Every experience teaches you something. Capture the lessons learned from this relationship and add it to your toolkit for managing relationships.

Remember that ending a professional relationship amicably shows maturity, professionalism, and respect for the other person. It reflects positively on your character and can contribute to a positive reputation in your industry or field.

I once had to sever a relationship with a business partner. If I'm to be honest in retrospect, from the get-go, I knew the CEO and I didn't have the same values, but I didn't know then what I know now. From the beginning, there were hints of a condescending attitude and feeling towards me and my company. Snide comments about us being a one-person company, even though I had employees at our first meeting. Once we started working together, everything was fine as long as we didn't have to interact much, and there was no crisis. Then the customer faced budget cuts, and we had to make some changes to the team, and they became inflexible and very difficult to work with; they undermined us because they had more experience, even though we were the prime contractor. Remember people will default to what they believe when they are unguarded and in crisis. That crisis let me know that they were not a true partner indeed. And we amicably severed ties after a year.

Still having not learned the lesson, I went back to team with them a year after that on another opportunity because of their experience and industry credentials, and the experience of putting this bid together with them was worse than what I experienced before. I prayed we would not get the contract, so I wouldn't have to work with them, not because they were bad people, but because our values did not align. On paper, we looked like a formidable team, but in reality, we could not coexist. This is a perfect example of when to cut ties if necessary; when you experience negativity in different capacities with the same group and the competence level is high, it's time to go because it is a values issue.

PART III

LEADING IN AN ORGANIZATION

7

NAVIGATING AN
ORGANIZATION'S DYNAMICS

Once upon a time, there was a CEO named 'Juan', who took over a car repair workshop known for its chaotic and quirky organizational systems. On his first day, he entered the workshop and was greeted by employees wearing mismatched uniforms and a friendly office cat that seemed to have made the workshop its home.

"Welcome to our little corner of the automotive world," the receptionist said with a warm smile.

Eager to understand the workshop's complexities, Juan rolled up his sleeves and immersed himself in the daily operations. He soon discovered the workshop's filing system was more like a treasure hunt, with important repair records hidden in unexpected places.

"We can definitely improve this," he thought optimistically.

Next on Juan's agenda was change management. He scheduled a meeting with the entire team to introduce himself and share his vision for the workshop's future. However, just as he was about to start, a sudden power outage plunged the workshop into darkness. Remaining calm, Juan led everyone outside while they waited for the electricity to be restored.

In the following days, Juan learned that dealing with complexities in the workshop meant untangling a web of quirky processes. One of the mechanics, Miguel, was known for his practical jokes, often sneaking funny notes into the toolboxes of his colleagues. Juan decided to play along and joined in the laughter when he discovered a "You've been pranked!" note in his own toolbox.

As Juan navigated the workshop's idiosyncrasies, he also discovered hidden talents among the mechanics. Rosa, one of the experienced mechanics, was a skilled salsa dancer, and Carlos, the youngest member of the team, had a talent for solving Rubik's cubes in record time.

"We have a truly diverse and talented team," Juan marveled.

Despite the initial chaos, Juan recognized the passion and potential in his team. He implemented new systems to streamline repair processes, fostered open communication, and encouraged creativity. Slowly but surely, the workshop's quirky charm merged with efficient practices.

One day, a potential client visited the workshop to discuss a major fleet repair contract. Juan had prepared for weeks, ensuring the workshop was at its best. But just as the meeting was about to begin, the friendly office cat decided to take a leisurely stroll across the conference table. The room shared a collective smile, and Juan gracefully continued with the presentation.

To his delight, the potential client was charmed by the workshop's unique atmosphere and saw it as a refreshing change from the typical corporate garages. The partnership was sealed with a firm handshake and a promise to send the office cat a "thank you" treat.

As time went on, Juan's leadership and adaptability transformed the workshop into a place where organized creativity and innovation thrived. The workshop's reputation as a reliable and friendly repair destination spread, attracting new customers and word-of-mouth referrals.

And so, with a mix of change management, crisis management, and a touch of warmth, Juan led the workshop to new heights. He realized that sometimes, the key to navigating complexities is embracing the unique character that sets an organization apart. And they all thrived, working together in harmony, under the watchful eye of the friendly office cat.

Organizations are intricate and dynamic entities designed to achieve specific goals or fulfill a purpose. They represent a convergence of people, processes, and technology, all working in unison to create a functioning whole. Whether they are mechanic workshops, nonprofit organizations, private entities, academic institutions, or publicly owned businesses, organizations are complex systems that take on the nature of their founders, leaders, and stakeholders. Leading an organization requires specific skills, awareness, and experience, depending on the nature and complexities involved in the organization.

Juan was a new leader and had to first determine the dynamics of the workshop, identify areas of improvement, score the talent of his human resources, implement change, and grow. While implementing change, he did not change the essence of the organization, like its more laid-back culture and the presence of the workshop cat. This is what you do as the first one when you lead an organization.

As the first one, you perform your duties as a leader within an organization. Whether it is a large organization, like a federal agency with thousands of employees, multiple policies, regulations, processes, programs, and stakeholders, or a small business with two employees, you lead in the context of a system, an organization, an entity. So, once you master leading yourself and leading people, you then must master leading the organization itself. In this story, Juan uses his personal leadership competency and expertise in motivating and influencing people to steer a disorganized workshop to a new direction of prosperity and new heights.

It is important for emerging leaders to understand the organization is an entity and has its own identity, culture, nature, structure. If the leader is the driver/builder, people are the engine/motor, and the organization is the vehicle itself that carries the leader and the people to their destination. Most first-time leaders struggle to understand this. They think the organization is this arbitrary thing on a piece of paper as business, policy, or corporate documents, a website, or name. An organization is an entity. The phrase "corporations are people" has been a topic of debate and controversy in the realm of corporate law and political discourse. The quote originated from a statement made by former Republican presidential candidate Mitt Romney during a campaign event in Iowa in 2011. The statement makes more sense in the context of an analogy because like people, corporations have interests, identities, cultures, goals, objectives, and a purpose. They exist for a reason. Also, the idea of corporate personhood, which is a legal concept, grants certain rights and protections to corporations, similar to those of individuals. For example, corporations have the right to enter contracts, own property, and sue or be sued in court. While it is important to know the ethical and legal distinctions between organizations and entities, leaders must understand the nature, components, and purpose of an organization to lead it well. All organizations exist for a purpose and are made up of people, a particular structure, and a culture.

ORGANIZATIONAL CULTURE

Organizational culture is a set of norms accepted and practiced by the people who work in it. Generally, organizations take on the culture and values of its leaders, power brokers, and decision makers. Every organization has a mission statement, vision statement, and values, but the culture of the organization is what the people in it experience because it is how they act towards one another. In the story of the workshop, you see Juan, a new leader, coming in to change the culture of the shop from a friendly, unorganized, and underperforming culture. There was no standard of conduct for the employees, their filing system had no rhyme or reason, and employees were not performing at their full potential. By using change management techniques, he implemented some policies and systems to drive efficiencies in the workshop and developed the unharnessed talent of the staff to improve their performance. He implemented this change while maintaining the friendly atmosphere that characterized the shop.

When you lead an organization, everything you say, do, and tolerate shapes the culture of the organization. Have you heard the saying, "Culture eats strategy for breakfast"? That is very true. Often, leaders are not able to meet their performance benchmarks because their organizational culture does not make it possible to do so. For example, you say in your strategic plan that you want to expand your reach into new sectors of the market, but your culture does not support innovation. While the strategic plan sounds good on paper, it most likely will not materialize because when ideas come in about how to enter new markets, those ideas are shut down. Expansion requires innovation, and innovation only happens with risk taking. If risk taking is not encouraged, expansion cannot occur.

As leadership consultants, my team often conducts assessments of organizational climates; we ask questions about people's perceptions of their work, their role in the organization, whether they feel supported, and whether they are allowed to make decisions, and it is always startling to see the delta between what leadership thinks is happening in their organization and what is actually happening. Some leaders are so out of touch with the actual culture of their organization that when faced with the data from these assessments, they shudder. Systemic issues in organizations such as low engagement, high turnover, and poor performance are rooted in culture. My business coach always asks me this question: "How does a fish rot?" The answer is, from the head down.

In leading an organization, you must move with the awareness that you are a key factor in what your organization is. This is why your leadership philosophy is important. It will dictate what kind of culture you create.

Human Synergistics developed the most widely used culture assessment I know: the Organizational Culture Inventory (OCI), backed by fifty years of research; its research is from data from four continents, the only true global organizational culture assessment on the market. As a credentialed practitioner of the OCI, I use this assessment to determine an organization's current culture state and desired state, and I design actions to move the organization to its desired state. Generally, organizational cultures are either constructive or destructive on a spectrum of behavior norms; constructive behavior norms enable employees to thrive and perform at a high level, while destructive behavior norms, whether passive or aggressive, stifle employees and create low performance and productivity.

There are other culture assessments on the market that can help you determine the current state of your organizational culture. As the first one, understanding the state of your organizational culture should be a priority, so that you know how to move. Organizational culture climate is like the weather; when it's warm, you dress lightly, but when it's cold, you add layers. As an emerging leader, knowing your organizational culture will help you determine how to execute your leadership philosophy and expose areas of improvement you can target within the organization. If you are a new leader, you may not be responsible for creating the current culture in your organization, but you have a significant role in reshaping it.

Knowing your organization's culture will help you understand its identity. Remember that organizations are entities, with distinct characteristics. In understanding your organization's identity, you must know the real organizational chart, know the power brokers, people who possess power and exchange it for benefit, and decision makers, people with authority to make major decisions. Don't focus on title, ranks, grades, or the size of their office; focus on what they can deliver. A receptionist with strong personal ties to the CEO, who manages the CEO's calendar, is a stronger power broker than a director under the CEO who is not trusted. If you don't remember anything else, in understanding an organization, please understand this: You must know the power brokers and decision makers within the organization you want to have an influence in.

Power brokers are influential individuals in the organization who hold significant sway over matters. They utilize their authority, connections, and resources to shape decisions and outcomes in their favor. Operating across various domains, such as policy, operations, and budget, power brokers engage in a range of activities to exert their influence. In large bureaucracies, they focus on budget and policy decisions.

Their core strategy is building and leveraging extensive networks of contacts, including influential individuals, stakeholders, and decision-makers. These networks grant them access to crucial information, enabling them to influence decisions and advance their own interests and the interests of their alliances. Skilled negotiators, power brokers leverage their influence to strike favorable deals, form alliances, and secure agreements that benefit themselves or their constituents.

Power brokers are also skilled at shaping public opinion; they often control or influence messaging to achieve their aim. Through meetings, presentations, speaking engagements, and other outreach mechanisms, they promote their interests, discredit opponents, and control the flow of information. Furthermore, power brokers excel at fundraising and resource mobilization, amassing substantial financial resources to support their initiatives or favored allies.

During times of conflict, power brokers may act as mediators, leveraging their influence to facilitate negotiations and find compromises that serve their own interests. This is a tactic that increases their influence in the organization because people see them as solution providers, mentors, problem solvers, and elders. Outside the organization, they engage in lobbying and advocacy efforts to influence legislation and government policies, working behind the scenes to shape laws and regulations to the advantage of their organizations. Large organizations have senior executives with strong relationships with local, state, and federal bodies for this purpose.

Another tactic employed by power brokers involves securing key appointments within government, organizations, or institutions, which grants them additional influence from within. In government contracting, many successful firms hire former senior government officials. They play golf together; their kids go to the same schools. They leverage these relationships to get access to information about procurements the average person will never have. Some power brokers resort to coercion, pressure tactics, or intimidation to achieve their goals, using their influence to threaten legal action, expose scandals, or damage reputations. This game is played in every organization, big or small. In some organizations, the game is subtle because of the culture, but in other organizations, the game is overt.

Exploiting information asymmetry is another tool in their arsenal. Power brokers may possess privileged information that others lack, allowing them to gain an upper hand in negotiations or decision-making processes. They play a significant role in setting agendas and determining which issues receive attention and resources.

To bolster their influence, power brokers nurture alliances and coalitions with like-minded individuals and groups. Additionally, they provide patronage to individuals and organizations that support their interests, extending financial support, endorsements, or other forms of assistance.

It is crucial to recognize that power brokers can have positive or negative influence in an organization. One of the deadliest things that can happen to a new leader is to be on the wrong side of a major power broker within the organization. They can cripple you. No matter how talented you are, how much leadership presence you have, or your capacity, a power broker can take you down in an organization. As an emerging leader, you must know who they are in your organization and develop yourself to be one. Yes, you must be a power broker yourself. You cannot lead an organization without being a power broker.

In my opinion, there is no greater power broker than Nancy Pelosi. I have read many books written about her, and I have studied her more than any other woman leader. Nancy Pelosi is a prominent American politician and a notable power broker in the US Congress. Born on March 26, 1940, in Baltimore, Maryland, she began her political career in the Democratic party and has since become one of its most influential figures. People underestimate how difficult it is to lead in a polarized government as woman. Pelosi's political journey has been marked by numerous accomplishments, earning her the distinction of being the first woman to serve as Speaker of the US House of Representatives.

As a seasoned power broker, she is a master in building and leveraging networks. The political pundits often ponder her ability to get her folks in the Democratic party, who are often on various spectrums of the issues, in line and garner their votes. She has forged strong alliances with key players both in her party and across the aisle, making her an adept negotiator and dealmaker in Congress. Pelosi always has the votes. This is incredible, as we have witnessed other speakers in the other party resign after a few years due to their inability to get votes and secure deals. Throughout her tenure, Pelosi was instrumental in pushing forward legislative agendas and securing critical compromises on various issues. What I love most about her is her style. As a petite woman, it is easy to underestimate her; her soft-spoken nature can be mistaken for weakness, but if you listen to her and watch her closely, you'll see her no-nonsense attitude makes her a winner.

Pelosi's influence is not only limited to her own party but also extends to the media landscape. As a savvy communicator, she has utilized media platforms to shape public opinion and advocate for her policy priorities. Her skillful use of media has earned her a reputation as a strategic communicator, able to convey her message effectively and mobilize support. During the Trump presidency, her use of media was masterful. When she wanted to announce the impeachment of the president, it was carefully curated. She knew how to make the media tell the story she wanted to tell. As a power broker, Pelosi's influence is formidable, and her political acumen has solidified her place as one of the most influential figures in American politics. With a career spanning decades and a reputation for strategic decision-making, she remains a key player in shaping the trajectory of the nation's legislative agenda.

Power brokers control the dynamics of an organization. As a leader of an organization, you want to grow from knowing the game and the players within the organization to writing the code for the game and picking the players. Some people see this as a negative thing; remember, brokering power can be used for good or bad. Your intention for controlling the dynamics of the organization you lead must be for the good of your team and the organization, not for manipulative purposes.

How do you become a power broker, you ask? Here are some ideas I'd like you to consider: Becoming a power broker in an organization is a journey that demands a strategic and purposeful approach. It involves a series of deliberate steps to cultivate influence and make a lasting impact within the company. Here's how one might embark on this path:

First, recognize the importance of building a strong network. Start by establishing and nurturing connections within and beyond the organization. Attend industry events, conferences, and networking functions for the opportunity to meet influential individuals and decision-makers. Your aim should be to foster genuine relationships based on trust and mutual benefit, laying the groundwork for future collaborations. Don't meet people and start selling to them or talking about your business or asking for a favor. That is a turn-off. Get to know the person and their interests, get into their world, and make yourself valuable. Position yourself as someone they want to have a relationship with; show how it benefits them.

Next, focus on showcasing your expertise and leadership abilities. To become a power broker, you must strive to become an expert in your field, gaining a deep understanding of industry trends, challenges, and opportunities. By sharing insights through thought leadership, speaking engagements, or publishing articles, you position yourself as a respected voice in the industry. After I left government service, to build my credibility in the government contracting industry, I taught a series of courses on small business programs for the small business development centers (SBDC) across the state of Maryland. I did not get paid to teach these courses, but I was intentionally showcasing my expert understanding of small business programs for federal contracting. I quickly became known for helping business get certified in the small business programs, and my client list grew, but more than that, people came to me when they had complex application issues because they knew I had the depth of expertise to deal with it.

To become a power broker, you must sow the seeds of service. If I did not have the seed of service after over three years with the SBDC, I would not have reaped the fruit of being a thought leader in the government contracting space.

Also, be intentional about cultivating influence within your organization as a vital aspect of the journey of being a power broker. If you deliver impactful results and make significant contributions to the company's success, the decision makers will notice you. Take on challenging projects and lead cross-functional teams; showcase your ability to drive positive change within the organization. Decision makers don't want to have to execute. They love leaders who make them look good. They gravitate towards leaders who produce. Whenever you deliver excellent results for a decision maker, you are building leverage.

In AMA Consulting, I have several project managers, but there is one who has built leverage with me, and she uses that leverage in a way that others can't. Why? She delivers. She is excellent at what she does, she is always helpful, and she is the project manager who has brought the most new business into the company. She does have leverage with me because she is very valuable to the organization and a support to me, the leader. Don't be the leader no one remembers when you're not there. Deliver results, and you will quickly become a power broker.

Steve Jobs said, "The most powerful person in the world is the storyteller." Being a power broker requires strong communication and persuasion skills. This is a crucial tool in your arsenal because every day, you are selling your skills, abilities, and potential deliverables to a skeptical audience in an organization. As the first one, people don't know what you can do; you must sell it. Work on articulating ideas clearly and persuasively; this is the way to ensure your initiatives gain the support they deserve. Prepare for meetings and learn how to deliver presentations in convincing ways that align with your leadership philosophy. You don't need to be obnoxious or boastful. There are some leaders who sing so much about what they do and work on their brand all day that it becomes their full-time job. Posting on social media every single achievement or pseudo achievement will not get you leverage; it will only get you admiration. Using social media to communicate your value and what you bring to an issue, program, or subject matter in a meaningful way helps you build leverage.

As you work to build leverage and become a power broker, align with key decision-makers and other power players in the organization; learn from them, study them, and know you are their equal. Build the confidence to approach them within the organization, eye to eye. Never approach them as a lesser person. Understand their priorities, interests, and pain points so you can tailor proposals and initiatives to align with their objectives. This will increase the likelihood of gaining their support. Form alliances with like-minded individuals and build coalitions. This will increase your influence. Collaborate with colleagues and stakeholders to achieve shared goals. This demonstrates your ability to work effectively as a team player. You can't build leverage as an island; you need strong support and alliances to be fortified within your organization. I have coached many leaders who struggled due to not having strong coalitions within the organization. I coached a leader who was blindsided when her portfolio shrunk 50 percent in a reorganization. She was blindsided because she didn't have an informant to let her know what was coming or advocate to secure a beneficial outcome for her when these decisions were being made.

Maintaining a positive reputation is paramount when you are developing as a power broker. Your reputation is how you earn respect. Do you keep your word? Do you use tact in dealing with issues? Do you exercise restraint? Power brokers are not loose mouthed and not easily angered. People trust and rely on leaders who are consistently humble, fair in their treatment of others, honest, steady, and professional. I worked with a leader who had a reputation for being a loudmouth. Everyone knew he couldn't keep a secret. Senior leaders don't confide in people who mouth off their ideas or considerations when it is not yet a solidified plan. He started being excluded from certain conversations because he couldn't be trusted to restrain his words. You have to be intentional about your reputation as a leader. Always know how people experience you or, as I like to say, what the word on the street is about you. When I worked at the US Small Business Administration, my district director would always ask me what the people were saying about her. I used to wonder why she cared so much. I was an emerging leader then and didn't understand that having situational awareness is key to managing your reputation within the organization. I do the same thing now in my company. I always take a pulse on how the team is experiencing me as a leader. Why? People talk;

they talk about their experience at work. If the talk is constantly negative, it undermines you and erodes your leverage. Your goal is for people to see the reputation you are putting out. You want them to experience your leadership philosophy. If they are experiencing something else, you need to know, and you need to know fast. If the reason for the delta between what you put out and what they experience is due to a communication gap; you need to work on it. If the reason is external like sabotage from someone damaging your reputation, you need to know and act fast.

Yes, an opponent within an organization can damage your reputation to sabotage you. This happens a lot in politics; politicians put out false stories about their opponents to damage their reputation and undermine their credibility. This happens in organizations too. People can subtly damage your reputation by mischaracterizing your position on issues, spreading false stories, or even just repeating an account of a situation or discussion in a negative way. You need to be conscious of that and take control of the narrative out there about you.

To be a power broker, you must be adaptable and resilient. Things change constantly within an organization, so you need to be malleable to take advantage of the changes. Decision makers come and go; power structure changes, so you must be nimble. Also, as a power broker, you will face challenges and stiff opposition, so you must be able to bounce back and maintain focus on objectives to persevere and achieve long-term success. Finally, recognize the importance of continuous learning and growth. Keep yourself updated on industry trends and best practices that will keep you ahead of the curve, ensure your relevance, and make you an influential figure in the organization. Becoming a power broker is not an overnight transformation; it requires patience, persistence, and a commitment to using influence for positive change and the collective success of the organization. By adopting these tips in a way that aligns with your leadership philosophy and staying true to your purpose, you will begin to lay the foundation and gain ground as a respected and impactful power broker in your organization.

In navigating the dynamic of an organization, you must gain the confidence of decision makers. Decision makers are those responsible for making choices and determining courses of action in a particular context. In organizations, decision makers are those who have the authority or responsibility to analyze information, weigh options, and select the best course of action among available alternatives.

In any organization, decision makers hold a pivotal role in steering its direction and achieving its goals. As a leader or an individual navigating within the dynamic of an organization, understanding the concepts of authority and responsibility is crucial in gaining the confidence of decision makers and influencing positive outcomes.

Authority is the power or right bestowed upon a person or position to make decisions and take action. Decision makers in an organization typically possess the authority to make choices that affect various aspects of the organization, such as strategic planning, resource allocation, and policy implementation. Authority is bestowed on you; you cannot cultivate it. It is also finite. You either have it or you don't. In your role, you must know the limits of your power and accept that authority ends there. Even the president of the US, the greatest country in the world, does not have the authority to take certain actions without approval from Congress. This authority is derived from the scope of your position, governing documents of the organization, your expertise, or delegation from higher levels of leadership. It is essential that you recognize and respect the authority of decision makers within the organizational structure, as they hold the responsibility to shape the organization's course. Leaders who are very aspirational and creative may struggle with respecting the authority of other leaders. One of the ways to shoot yourself in the foot within an organization is to attempt an action and be pulled back because you never had the authority to take that action to begin with.

Responsibility, on the other hand, refers to the obligation and accountability that decision makers have toward the outcomes of their choices. As they weigh options and select courses of action, decision makers must consider not only the potential benefits but also the risks and consequences of their decisions. Their responsibility extends beyond their own interests to encompass the well-being of the organization, its stakeholders, and sometimes even the broader community. Demonstrating an understanding of this responsibility and supporting decision makers in fulfilling their duties can foster a positive working relationship. One way to become close to decision makers is to take things off their plate. People underestimate how much decision makers need support because of the weight of the responsibility they carry. Here are a few ways to support a decision maker and establish yourself as a valuable asset to them:

Take the time to understand the decision maker's priorities and objectives. Engage in open conversations and actively listen to their concerns, challenges, and goals. This understanding will help you align your initiatives and actions with their vision for the organization. Remember that decision makers are people. They have worries, struggles, and aspirations, and most times, they also have a boss, board, or constituents to answer to. Spend time listening to the initiative briefings, understand the why behind their actions, and show them you are really interested in what they are seeking to achieve. Remember the law of reciprocity. You have something they want: compassion. Show it by taking the time to understand their priorities.

Beyond showing them you care, give them tangible information that can help them make good decisions. Decision makers appreciate well-informed and data-driven insights. Provide them with relevant data, market trends, and comprehensive analyses to help them make informed choices. If you work with a senior leader who has to make a presentation on a matter and do research and present him/her with some talking points in the form of data, you will quickly become a trusted advisor.

As a leader, nothing gives me more joy than when I have something on my plate and someone on my team has proactively handled it without me asking. The relief I experience is great. Decision makers often manage multiple polarities in their roles, and they have a long to-do list. Anticipate the needs and requirements of decision makers and take proactive steps to address potential issues or opportunities; this establishes you as a strategic thinker with the decision maker because in order to anticipate, you had to have foresight, research the issue, address it, and then communicate it to the decision maker. In being proactive, ensure you are taking action within your scope of authority and the boundaries of the decision maker. Seize on conversations and hints to identify opportunities to take action that helps them, but don't be too forward. If you have studied this decision maker, you'll know when an opportunity arises to be proactive. Being proactive showcases your initiative and dedication to supporting the organization's success.

BE SOLUTION-ORIENTED

Decision makers will shut you out if you are in the habit of asking them something you should know or bringing problems without possible solutions. It shows professional immaturity. When presenting a problem to a decision maker, present the problem, its effects, possible solution options, and pros and cons of each option. This is a solutions-oriented approach to presenting issues for a decision maker to deliberate on. In politics, lawmakers have staffers; this is their job. They read the proposed bills, collect public view of each, research the effect and cost of the bill, and the lawmaker provides direction on the bill based on their expertise. As a leader, get your staff to thoroughly vet an issue and research possible solutions before you present that issue to a decision maker. A solution-oriented approach shows you are a problem solver and can be relied upon to handle difficulties effectively.

As a leader, you are also a decision maker. When you are new to an organization as a leader, you must identify senior decision makers within your organization and manage the authority and responsibilities you have. Steward them well. Michelle Obama said, "Managing authority means leading with fairness, transparency, and a commitment to the greater good." Your job is to understand the scope of your authority, act within that scope, and take on your responsibility. Understanding the scope of your authority is a critical aspect of effective leadership. As a new leader, you must be aware of the limits and extent of your decision-making power to make well-informed choices and avoid overstepping boundaries. Here are some tips to help you in this area:

Familiarize yourself with the formal and informal organizational chart and hierarchy. Understand your place within the larger structure and how it relates to other departments and teams. Identify the reporting lines and levels of decision-making authority. If you work in a bureaucracy, review your organization's policy and HR rules. Thoroughly review your job description and role expectations. Before you take on any leadership role, ensure that you understand what you will be held accountable for. As things evolve in your role, and you assume more responsibilities or relinquish some, check with your organization for understanding. This will give you insights into the responsibilities and tasks assigned to you. It will also help you understand what areas are under your direct control and where you need to collaborate with other teams or leaders. Determine who you report to and who reports to you. Understand the flow of information and decision-making within the organization. This clarity will help you navigate the chain of command and avoid unnecessary conflicts.

Once you know the boundaries of your authority, be fair and never abuse your authority. We've all heard the phrase "power intoxicates." That's true, but I say it only intoxicates insecure leaders who want to lead only for their personal gain. Abraham Lincoln said, "Nearly all men can stand adversity, but if you want to test a man's character, give him power."

Power only amplifies who you really are. Power makes you act out what you truly believe. If you understand that the authority you have is for the good of your team and the organization, you will steward it with humility and fairness. History records stories of great leaders who fell because of their abuse of power. One such true-life story is that of Richard Nixon, the thirty-seventh president of the United States. Nixon was a prominent leader who achieved many successes during his political career but was also plagued by a deep intoxication with authority that eventually led to his downfall.

Nixon rose to power in the late 1960s and was reelected as president in 1972. He was known for his political cunning, intelligence, and determination. However, during his presidency, Nixon became increasingly obsessed with maintaining control and suppressing perceived threats to his authority.

The Watergate scandal is the event that marked Nixon's downfall. In 1972, a group of men associated with Nixon's reelection campaign was caught breaking into the Democratic National Committee headquarters at the Watergate complex in Washington DC. The initial break-in was an attempt to wiretap phones and gather intelligence on Nixon's political opponents.

As investigations into the break-in intensified, evidence emerged linking the break-in to the Nixon administration. It was revealed that Nixon's aides had engaged in a cover-up to conceal their involvement and to obstruct the investigation. The scandal escalated as the media and public demanded answers about Nixon's knowledge and role in the cover-up.

Nixon's intoxication with authority and his obsession with maintaining power led him to authorize illegal activities and abuse the power of his office. Instead of acknowledging the wrongdoing and taking responsibility, Nixon tried to evade accountability and distance himself from the scandal.

As pressure mounted, Nixon eventually faced impeachment proceedings in the US House of Representatives. Faced with the likelihood of impeachment and removal from office, he made the historic decision to resign from the presidency on August 8, 1974. Nixon became the first and, to this day, the only US president to resign from office.

The Watergate scandal left a profound impact on American politics and governance. It exposed the dangers of unchecked authority and the importance of transparency, accountability, and ethical leadership in government. Nixon's legacy remains tarnished by his abuse of authority, but the scandal also served as a powerful reminder of the need for leaders to act with integrity and humility.

There are other things to keep in mind regarding authority, such as ethics and legalities. In most situations, there are policies and regulations that confer authority on a leader, and a breach means an ethics violation or, even more severe, a violation of the law. Always err on the side of caution with your decision-making to maintain ethics and uphold the law; your decisions must pass the security of the public eye. My mom always told me while growing up, "Never do anything privately and not own up to it publicly". I will share this piece of wisdom with you. Be upright in your decision-making and be transparent. It will save you from having to cover up and look over your shoulder, and when you're transparent, you close the opening for your opponents to sabotage you.

I watched an interview recently with Michelle Obama and Oprah Winfrey; there was a point in their conversation where Oprah praised Obama for not slipping once during her tenure as first lady; she said she was proud of her. As the first black first lady, Mrs. Obama's opponents would have eaten her for lunch if there was even a sliver of impropriety on her part in her role. We who belong to the exclusive group of others or minorities have it tougher. We cannot give room for any attacks. I personally don't think it's fair, but it is the reality, and as the first one, I want to let you know, the first time you have an accident or make a mistake, they will come for you. I don't need to tell you who they are; you already know.

Leaders do not pass the buck. Winston Churchill said, "The price of greatness is responsibility." As events occur within an organization, you can delegate tasks, but the buck ultimately stops with you. It is important for you to not pass the buck because doing so undermines trust, accountability, and team morale within the organization. When you don't take responsibility for your actions or decisions, it creates a culture of blame-shifting and finger-pointing, which can have several negative consequences, such as low performance and low motivation. Nothing reeks of immaturity like a leader who will not take responsibility for anything. Good or bad, always own up and fess up. The price you pay for the perks of leadership is responsibility. Avoiding responsibility as a leader is like wanting to be a captain without a rudder. The ship will go astray.

Organizations are complex. They have different identities based on size, structure, culture. Organizations take on the identity of their leaders and work toward a particular purpose. Every organization has a game that is played daily, and the stars of this game are the power brokers and decision makers. To lead an organization effectively, you must understand the dynamics, wield power for the good of your people and the system, and bear the burden of the responsibility of leadership.

8

DRIVING ORGANIZATIONAL PERFORMANCE

Every organization has a clear purpose or set of goals that guides its existence. Nonprofit organizations aim to address social or environmental issues, private businesses strive for profitability and market presence, while academic institutions focus on education and research. The organization's purpose serves as a guiding light, directing its decisions, strategies, and resource allocation. As a leader of an organization, you must know what your organization's purpose is and how your role helps to achieve it. This is easy if you work in a small business, or you've started a nonprofit on your own. It becomes infinitely challenging when you lead a large organization with layers of bureaucracy and multiple levels of authority and department. What is the measure of success for your organization? How will you know that your organization is achieving its mission and fulfilling the need it was created to fulfil? As the leader of this organization, you must know the answer to these questions. How can you do this? Organizational leaders must engage in strategic planning. There is a saying that if you don't know where you're going, any road will take you there. Jack Welch, former CEO of General Electric, said, "Strategic planning is a compass that helps navigate the storms and seize the opportunities in a rapidly changing world."

Strategic planning is a structured map that gives direction to organizational goals. It ensures that all departments, divisions, and teams are working in alignment toward the mission of the organization. Some leaders feel that strategic plans are just fancy documents consultants charge exorbitant amounts to develop, while other leaders see a strategic plan as a living document that guides the entire organization and provides marching orders, like a GPS. Beyond the plan, which is the document, the strategic planning process offers great value to leaders. Planning often includes conducting trend analyses and reviewing organizational assessment information from strength, weakness, opportunity, and threat (SWOT) analyses, employee engagement data, and competitor information. This exercise is culminated in a planning session with senior leaders to brainstorm and set goals and objectives for the organization. The planning process also includes setting performance metrics and evaluation mechanisms. This process helps leaders assess the current state of the organization, identify potential opportunities and threats, and determine the future state they want the organization to achieve.

Smaller organizations often fail because they don't have regular strategic planning. Most small business owners start their companies and strive for growth, but they rarely develop a map for the organization to get to its desired state. This is because small business owners are so preoccupied with surviving and growing, they neglect planning, when planning is the key to sustained growth.

Not having a strategic plan can lead to several disadvantages and challenges for an organization, such as the following:

1. **Lack of Direction:** Without a strategic plan, an organization lacks a clear direction and long-term vision. This can result in a lack of focus and purpose, with employees unsure of what they are working toward.
2. **Reactive Decision-Making:** Without a strategic plan to guide decision-making, the organization may be forced to react to immediate issues and crises without considering the long-term implications.

3. **Resource Misallocation:** Without a strategic plan, resources such as time, money, and personnel may be misallocated, leading to inefficiencies and wasted opportunities.
4. **Missed Opportunities:** Without a strategic plan, the organization may miss out on potential opportunities for growth and improvement.
5. **Lack of Alignment:** Without a strategic plan, individual departments or teams may operate in silos, leading to a lack of alignment and coordination across the organization.
6. **Increased Risk:** Not having a strategic plan leaves the organization vulnerable to unexpected challenges and risks, without a proactive plan for managing and mitigating them.
7. **Reduced Accountability:** Without the clear goals and objectives of a strategic plan, it can be challenging to hold employees accountable for their performance and results.
8. **Decline in Competitiveness:** Without a strategic plan, the organization may struggle to keep up with competitors who have well-defined strategies and plans for growth.
9. **Decreased Employee Engagement:** Without a strategic plan, employees may feel disconnected from the organization's mission and goals, leading to decreased motivation and engagement.
10. **Inefficient Operations:** The absence of a strategic plan can lead to inefficient operations and faulty decision-making processes, hindering the organization's ability to achieve its objectives.
11. **Short-Term Focus:** Without a strategic plan, the organization may prioritize short-term gains over long-term sustainability, compromising its future success.

If you are a small business owner and your organization is experiencing any of these challenges, practice an annual planning exercise, and you will begin to mitigate these issues. Not having a strategic plan can leave the organization adrift, lacking a clear sense of direction and purpose. It can result in missed opportunities, increased inefficiencies, and a lack of alignment, ultimately hindering the organization's ability to achieve its full potential and thrive in a competitive environment.

As a small business owner, I go through a planning exercise every year. In fact, I curated a conference to help small business federal government contractors plan for the new year; that conference has morphed into a full-day event called the Magnificent Leadership Conference. When I first started AMA Consulting, I conducted assessments and developed the organizational goals myself, with performance metrics. Our strategic plan has always been a one-pager. As we grew, I enlisted senior leaders in the planning process, and now we hire an outside consultant to help with our annual plan. Depending on the size and complexity of an organization, the planning process can be simple or elaborate. Generally, your planning process should include a variation of the following key steps to develop a comprehensive and effective strategy for your organization. The steps may vary depending on the specific context and needs of your organization, but the general process includes the following:

1. **Vision and Mission:** Define the organization's vision, which outlines its long-term aspirations and what it aims to achieve in the future. Establish the mission, which is the core purpose of the organization and why it exists.

2. **Situational Analysis:** Conduct a thorough analysis of the internal and external environment. This involves assessing the organization's strengths, weaknesses, opportunities, and threats (SWOT analysis). It also includes analyzing market trends, customer preferences, competitive landscape, and other factors that may affect your organization.

3. **Goal Setting:** Based on the vision and situational analysis, set specific and measurable goals and objectives for each focus area your organization wants to improve. Examples of a focus area can be operations, financial, and employee satisfaction. These goals should be aligned with the organization's mission and should be specific, measurable, achievable, realistic, and must have a timeline of completion (SMART).

4. **Strategy Formulation:** Facilitate sessions with leaders and stakeholders to consider various approaches, examine the options, and choose the most suitable strategies that leverage the organization's strengths, address its weaknesses, observe external opportunities, and assess threats.

5. **Development of Key Performance Indicators (KPIs):** Decide on metrics to measure success or achievement for each goal.

6. **Action Plan:** Create a detailed action plan that outlines the specific steps, timelines, and responsibilities for implementing the chosen strategies. This plan should include clear milestones and performance indicators to track progress.

7. **Resource Allocation:** Determine the resources required to implement the action plan successfully. This includes financial resources, human resources, new technology, and other necessary inputs.

8. **Implementation:** Execute the action plan by mobilizing resources, assigning responsibilities, and actively carrying out the identified strategies.

9. **Monitoring and Evaluation:** Regularly monitor the progress of the strategic plan and evaluate its effectiveness. Use key performance indicators to measure success and identify areas for improvement.

10. **Adaptation and Flexibility:** Be prepared to adapt the strategic plan as needed in response to changes in the internal or external environment. Flexibility is essential to respond to unexpected challenges or new opportunities.

11. **Communication and Engagement:** Communicate the strategic plan to all stakeholders, including employees, customers, investors, and partners. Engage stakeholders throughout the process to foster support and ensure commitment to the strategy.

12. **Continuous Improvement:** Strategic planning is an ongoing process. Continuously review and refine the strategic plan to ensure its relevance and effectiveness in achieving the organization's goals.

By following these steps, organizations can develop a robust and well-informed strategic plan. Here are some general rules of thumb when going through the planning process: Enlist outside help if you can. It always helps to have a neutral party conduct the organizational assessments and keep you, the leader, honest when it comes to goal setting. Decide on a few goals at a time. I recommend no more than three major goals annually, with five objectives under each goal. Ambitious leaders love to boil the ocean. You can do three things very well or do seven things marginally well. Review performance indicators periodically and adjust the plan. While a strategic plan will not stop the waves of change from altering your course as a leader of an organization, it serves as a guide to help you extract opportunities from the waves of change and not be destroyed by them.

The implementation of a strategic plan is what births organizational performance. This is how well an organization utilizes its resources to achieve its mission and satisfy its customers' needs. If you are a founder, the organization's mission, goals, and objectives originate from you initially, but if you work for a large organization, the mission, goals, and objective of the organization may not be totally dependent on you, the leader. I have seen the first ones struggle to change the goals and objectives of an organization they were hired to lead, without consensus from senior decision makers. That exercise is futile. I coached a leader who was newly hired as a branch chief into a more traditional government agency from a more progressive one. Upon hire, he attempted to change the objectives of the branch to be more progressive and far reaching. He was shut down and was almost frustrated out of the job. In determining the metrics for performance, you have to consider the people, structure, dynamics, and culture of the organization. Understand the landscape first, know what results the organization has been producing, and see what impacts were derived from those results. Investigate what is missing or needed from the target population the organization serves before you start to change performance metrics.

As a new leader, you will quickly learn that planning is easy in theory, but executing that plan requires a specific set of actions and decisions. In driving organizational performance, Thomas Edison said, "Vision without execution is just a hallucination."

Build a high-performing team. We have discussed leading people from a broad perspective, but to execute, you need doers. You need a high-performing team. Building a high-performing team requires a deliberate and strategic approach. Here are some key steps to create and foster a team that produces excellent results:

1. **Recruit and Develop the Right Talent:** Most emerging leaders struggle with ascertaining potential candidates' competencies related to the job requirement. Job descriptions are as worthless

as resumes; these documents only tell half the story. As a leader, you really need to know the work and what it requires from a potential hire, professionally, technically, and emotionally. Then you have to vet candidates on these three criteria, which is very difficult to do. Here are some tips that have helped: Avoid cookie-cutter job descriptions. Be as detailed as possible describing the job and the professional, ethical, and emotional requirements of the job. If possible, hire from referrals; conduct simple personality assessments and technical tests of candidates and ask for work samples. Hire team members with the right skills and qualities to complement each other. Look for a mix of expertise, experience, and diverse perspectives. Additionally, invest in training and development to enhance team members' capabilities.

2. **State Goals and Expectations:** Once your team is in place, state expectations openly and define a clear vision and set of goals for the team. Leaders often assume people know what to do and know what they want and how they want deliverables. This is wrong. Communicate this vision to all team members so everyone understands the direction and purpose of their work.

3. **Set Targets:** Clearly define roles and responsibilities for each team member and set weekly and monthly targets aligned with key performance indicators of the organization. Also leave room for contingencies so team members have room to be creative. Leaders often struggle with holding workers accountable, so clear targets eliminate ambiguity on the team. Also, ensure that each person's skills and strengths align with their roles.

4. **Build an Environment with Psychological Safety:** Trust is essential for high-performing teams. Establish trust by being reliable, honest, and supportive. Create a safe environment where team members feel comfortable taking risks and sharing their thoughts, without fear of judgment or repercussions. A psychologically safe environment motivates people to produce more. Encourage open and transparent communication within the team. Foster a culture where team members feel comfortable sharing their ideas, concerns, and feedback. Regular team meetings and updates can help ensure everyone is on the same page.

5. **Empower Decision-Making:** Delegate decision-making authority to team members when appropriate. Empowering team members to make decisions within their areas of expertise can increase engagement and ownership. Team members who take ownership of the work are more committed to achieving targets.

6. **Promote Collaboration:** Foster a collaborative culture where team members work together, share ideas, and help each other succeed. Encourage cross-functional collaboration, recognize new partnerships, and reward teamwork. This helps your team have high productivity with less stress.

7. **Provide Resources and Support:** Ensure the team has the necessary resources, tools, and support to achieve their goals. Remove any barriers or obstacles that may hinder their performance. Know what your team needs, and provide it. Don't give excuses when it comes time to deliver on a promise.

8. **Reciprocate when Your Team Delivers:** Recognize and celebrate team achievements, both big and small. Acknowledging individual and team successes boosts morale and reinforces a culture of excellence. Remember the theory of reciprocity. As your team delivers results, give them public praise, recognition, and tangible rewards in exchange.

9. **Continuous Improvement:** Encourage a mindset of continuous improvement. Regularly seek feedback from team members, and use it to identify areas for growth and development. Never waste mistakes or errors; empower your team to gain something new from them.

10. **Handle Conflicts Constructively:** Address conflicts and disagreements within the team promptly and constructively. Encourage open dialogue to resolve issues and find mutually beneficial solutions. Teach your team to be comfortable with grey areas and manage opposing poles. Infighting within team members negatively affects performance.

11. **Lead by Example:** As the leader, embody the values and behaviors you want to see in your team. Your actions set the tone for the team's culture and performance. If you want a high-performing team, be a high-performing leader; produce results yourself.

Building a high-performing team is an ongoing process that requires attention, effort, and adaptability. If you invest in the right people, foster a positive and collaborative environment, and promote a culture of excellence, you can create a team that consistently delivers outstanding results.

MANAGING RESOURCES

As a leader, it is your role to provide and manage the resources required for high performance in your organization. Organizational resources are human, technological, and financial. We have discussed tips to build a high-performing team. But after building the team, you must manage that team well. As I have mentioned throughout this book, people are the greatest resource you have. You as a leader must learn the skills to manage your human resources to achieve high performance. Additionally, financial and technological resources are required to run an organization. As the leader, whether it is advocating for funding, seeking donors, yielding profit, or conducting technological components, you must know what your organization needs and know how to get it.

Managing business resources requires acumen. Business acumen refers to the ability to understand and interpret various business- and program-related situations, make informed decisions, and implement effective strategies to drive organizational success. It involves a combination of business knowledge, analytical thinking, and practical judgment. This skill enables you as a leader to navigate complex business challenges and seize opportunities. Most organizations today are facing budget shortfalls, limited resources, and hiring shortages. To lead an organization effectively, you must have the business acumen to identify the resources your organization needs, develop creative sources of those things, and apply those resources in the most advantageous way. For example, leaders may have great talent, but their high-performing team may not be delivering on its potential due to misappropriation of tasks, wrong focus, and limiting beliefs. Additionally, some leaders have great ideas but don't have the business acumen to procure the resources they need to execute them.

The cornerstone of improving your business acumen is having a sales mindset. The truth is, resources are scarce. That excellent candidate you want to hire has a job offer with another organization. The funding you need is in the hands of a decision maker who has competing priorities. Why should that employee come to work for you? And why should the decision maker award you the funds? Why should people choose you?

A lot of first-time leaders don't realize we are all selling something. Everyone in an organization is making a case for why their project, program, or product should get priority. If you are not selling in your organization, you are losing. You must sell your idea, program, product, or initiative to receive the necessary resources you need. No one is just going to give them to you. This involves effective communication, persuasive arguments, and building support from stakeholders. Here are some strategies to help you successfully pitch your ideas and secure the resources you need:

1. **Know the Source of the Resources You Need:** It may shock you to find out that most leaders don't know what resources are available to them or who allocates these resources within their organization. Study the budget of your organization. Know the decision makers in charge of approving technology purchases. Know the process of requesting training or signing up for benefits for your team. You cannot receive what you don't know belongs to you or what you don't ask for.

2. **Craft a Compelling Story:** Practice using stories and hard data to create a compelling story of why your business, program, or initiative should get priority when resources are allocated. Use confident and persuasive communication when presenting your ideas. Speak with enthusiasm and conviction to inspire confidence in your proposals.

3. **Clearly Define the Value:** Clearly articulate the value and benefits of your ideas or program. Explain how they will solve specific problems, drive growth, or improve efficiency. Use data and evidence to support your claims. Answer the question, what will people get if they choose to expend resources on your idea, project, or program?

4. **Address Potential Concerns:** Anticipate potential objections or concerns from decision makers allocating resources, and address them proactively. Be prepared to offer solutions and assurances to alleviate their doubts. Realize that in every organization, you have competitors; other people want the resources you need as well.

5. **Highlight the Return on Investment (ROI):** Demonstrate the return on investment of your ideas or programs. Show how the resources allocated will lead to positive outcomes and contribute to your organization's success. If applicable, showcase past successes or pilot programs to demonstrate the feasibility of your ideas and their impact.

6. **Involve Key Stakeholders:** Involve key stakeholders in the decision-making process early on. Seek their input and feedback to build support and buy-in for your ideas. Form relationships with power brokers in your organization who can advocate for you. Identify influential stakeholders who can champion your ideas and advocate on your behalf. Having allies within the organization can significantly increase your chances of receiving the resources you need.

7. **Create a Detailed Plan:** Provide a well-thought-out and detailed plan for implementing your ideas. Include timelines, milestones, and key performance indicators to show you have a clear roadmap for success. This demonstrates to decision makers that the resources will be put to good use and not wasted.

8. **Be Persistent and Patient:** Selling your ideas and securing resources may require persistence and patience. Be prepared to engage in ongoing discussions and follow-up as needed.

Once you secure the resources you need, you must prioritize them; understand the difference between what's important and what's urgent. You must balance between executing urgent projects (tasks required to be done daily) and important projects (those that make the most impact on mission). Prioritization is a fundamental aspect of effective resource management and strategic decision-making within an organization. By prioritizing activities and projects, you can direct your limited resources to where they can have the most significant impact and drive the organization toward its mission and goals. I have had days where it seems I spent most of my time putting out fires and never did meaningful work or produced a deliverable. This happens to the best of us, but it cannot be a daily occurrence. Scarce resources, such as time, money, and personnel, require careful allocation. By prioritizing high-impact activities and projects, you can maximize the efficient use of resources. This approach prevents spreading resources too thinly across numerous initiatives, leading to diluted efforts and reduced outcomes.

Emerging leaders who operate from a place of fear, who try to please decision makers, often fall into this trap; they're like hamsters spinning on a wheel. If you focus on looking good, being popular, and pleasing people, you will have your team throwing darts at the wall and hoping something will stick. Great leaders focus their efforts on just a few critical initiatives. A concentrated effort results in greater attention to detail, enhanced problem-solving, and improved chances of success. It also minimizes distractions and prevents teams from becoming overwhelmed with an excessive workload.

Identifying and prioritizing high-impact activities also allows leaders to assess potential risks more effectively. Risk management becomes more targeted, and contingency plans can be developed for critical projects, ensuring the organization is prepared for unforeseen challenges. Priorities may evolve over time due to changing circumstances or new opportunities. With a well-defined prioritization framework, leaders can adapt and reallocate resources as needed, ensuring the organization remains agile and responsive to dynamic environments.

Prioritizing and focusing on critical tasks requires practicing restraint as a leader. It also requires you to keep your strategic objectives visible as you execute daily tasks. When I first started my business, I was terrible at prioritizing. I always did a strategic plan and had good intentions to execute tasks according to plan, but once a shiny object like a potential opportunity that was not in alignment with our strategic goals came about, I would lose focus. Also, as a new business owner, I had anxiety about being able to continually get work to keep the business running. I would go into periods where I was just targeting any and everything, with the mindset that if I put enough proposals out there, something will stick at least once a month. Boy, was I wrong; my knee-jerk reaction to business development showed in the turnover of my staff and slow growth. It wasn't until I built the discipline to define our three core verticals of services and say no to everything else that was not in alignment that major doors began to open. Also, I realized that when I was not intentional about the type of work we went after as a company, we would win work with very low margins that required a heavy lift from the staff. So this did not help the company's bottom line.

If you are building an enterprise from the ground up, it is not uncommon to be spread out too thin at first and focus more on urgent tasks as opposed to the important. But as the first one, know that your venture will succeed; practice restraint in pivoting too frequently and doing too much at the same time. Understand that you might have to say 'no' to a small fish to make you ready to catch the big one. Work according to your strategy. This mindset will help you allocate the resources within your organization effectively to achieve a greater bottom line.

The most valuable resource we have as human beings is time, and technology helps us conserve that time and do more in a shorter amount. In leading an enterprise, you must have a technology strategy attached to all facets of your operation and product and service delivery. I'll take it a step further; in this age, not only should you have a technology strategy, but you must also have an automation strategy. Why? It adds to your competitive advantage. It is more likely than not that your peers and competitors are incorporating automation to their operations. Automation saves time and money, and increases your efficiency as an organization. In the organizational development space, consultants are using ChatGPT to design and develop training and session materials and cutting their billable hours considerably, only expending most of their hours on actual client face time. If you are not doing that, your price for engagements may become too high for the market. Companies are automating routine administrative tasks and HR functions. If you are not doing that, those costs will be higher for you and price you out of the market.

So as a leader in an organization, adopt cutting-edge methodologies and technology to increase outputs. Stay abreast of the latest advancements in your industry and related fields. Regularly attend industry conferences, workshops, and seminars, and encourage your team to do the same. This will help you uncover methodologies that save you time, save you money, and help you work smarter. This practice has benefited me greatly in business. Customers, consumers, and stakeholders define your performance not only by quality but by relevance. A key part of driving performance is not just doing the work excellently but being relevant in your field. Follow thought leaders and experts in the field to gain insights into emerging technologies and methodologies.

Leaders of organizations today must leverage technological advancements, create efficiencies, and drive up performance. In my industry, for example, we see a trend of government leveraging technology through modernization efforts to create efficiencies. There are several ways technology increases an organization's performance:

Automation: Advanced technologies, such as artificial intelligence and robotics, can automate repetitive and mundane tasks that were previously performed manually. Automation reduces the need for human intervention, speeds up processes, and minimizes errors, leading to increased efficiency. Automation tools can increase our organization's output, using fewer resources.

Data Analysis: Technology allows for faster and more accurate data collection and analysis. With data-driven insights, leaders can make informed decisions and optimize their operations for better efficiency.

Virtual Communication and Collaboration: Technological tools, such as email, instant messaging, and video conferencing, enable seamless communication and collaboration among team members and stakeholders, regardless of their physical location. This fosters faster decision-making and problem-solving processes, regardless of geographic location.

Cloud Computing: Cloud-based technologies provide flexible and scalable solutions for storing and accessing data, software, and applications. This reduces the need for physical infrastructure and allows for efficient resource allocation.

Supply Chain Management: Technology has revolutionized supply chain management by enabling real-time tracking of goods, inventory management, and demand forecasting. This streamlines logistics and reduces lead times, enhancing overall efficiency.

Digital Workflows: Digital workflows, enabled by technology, replace paper-based processes with electronic ones. This eliminates manual handling, reduces paperwork, and accelerates the flow of information, further improving efficiency.

Customer Service: Technological advancements have transformed customer service through chatbots, AI-powered virtual assistants, and online self-service portals. These tools provide quick and efficient customer support, increased satisfaction, and enhanced loyalty, without adding workforce costs.

Internet of Things (IoT): IoT devices and sensors collect and transmit real-time data, facilitating predictive maintenance, asset tracking, and resource optimization. This minimizes downtime and enhances operational efficiency.

Remote Work: Technology allows employees to work remotely, offering flexibility and better work-life balance. Remote work can lead to increased productivity, a reduction in company overhead for office space and supplies, reduced commute times for workers, and improved job satisfaction.

Personalization: Advanced technologies enable personalized customer experiences, tailoring products and services to individual preferences. This enhances customer satisfaction and drives efficiency by reducing wasted resources on irrelevant offerings.

Enhanced Decision-Making: Data analytics, AI, and machine learning enable faster and more accurate decision-making. Leaders can access insights and predictive models, making strategic choices with greater confidence and efficiency.

In addition to technology, the methodologies you use in your organization affect your performance. Every industry has standard methodologies used over the years and newer ones that produce better results. As a leader, part of your role is to decide on the methodology that works best for the results you want to accomplish. You should be working with your team to develop frameworks and systems for service delivery that are unique to your organization. These frameworks are part of your organization's artifacts and distinguishers. You can build these frameworks with cutting-edge methodologies and real-life experience of what works for your organization and customers. In government, the Office of Management and Budget sets maturity models for organizations in agencies. This office sets benchmarks and standards that an organization should have to meet each level of maturity, and agencies are scored against the benchmarks. This is because as an organization matures, it must have more distinct features and a recognizable framework for how it does its work. When leading an organization, it should be your top priority to mature your business model, framework, and systems the same way you work to develop your people. There are several operational methodologies available that organizations can adopt to increase efficiency in their processes and workflows. Most of these methodologies can be applied in any industry, for services or products, even though some are more appropriate for specific industries. Here are some examples:

1. **Lean Methodology:** Lean focuses on eliminating waste and streamlining processes to deliver value to customers with fewer resources. It emphasizes continuous improvement, visual management, and standardized work to achieve higher efficiency.

2. **Six Sigma:** Six Sigma uses data-driven approaches to reduce defects and variations in processes. It follows DMAIC (Define, Measure, Analyze, Improve, Control), a structured problem-solving methodology to identify root causes of inefficiencies and eliminate them.

3. **Agile Methodology:** Originally developed for software development, Agile has been adopted in various industries. It emphasizes iterative and incremental work, close collaboration between teams and customers, and responsiveness to changing requirements, leading to faster and more efficient project delivery.

4. **Total Quality Management (TQM):** TQM is a comprehensive approach that involves the entire organization in continuous improvement efforts. It focuses on customer satisfaction, employee involvement, and process excellence to achieve higher efficiency and quality.

5. **Kanban:** Kanban is a visual management method that uses cards or boards to track work items through various stages of a process. It helps teams visualize their workflow, identify bottlenecks, and optimize the flow of work, resulting in improved efficiency.

6. **Theory of Constraints (TOC):** TOC identifies and addresses the most significant constraint or bottleneck that limits overall system performance. By focusing efforts on removing constraints, organizations can increase efficiency and boost throughput.

7. **Business Process Reengineering (BPR):** BPR involves radical redesign of business processes to achieve dramatic improvements in performance, efficiency, and quality. It often involves eliminating nonessential steps, automating tasks, and reorganizing workflows.

8. **5S Methodology:** Originating from Japanese practices, 5S (Sort, Set in Order, Shine, Standardize, Sustain) focuses on workplace organization and cleanliness. By creating an organized and efficient workspace, teams can improve productivity and reduce waste.

9. **Just-In-Time (JIT):** JIT is a manufacturing methodology that aims to produce goods or deliver services exactly when needed, with minimal or no inventory. By reducing inventory carrying costs and waste, JIT increases efficiency.

10. **Value Stream Mapping (VSM):** VSM is a visual representation of a process that helps identify areas of inefficiency and waste. It provides insights into the end-to-end flow of value, enabling organizations to optimize processes for improved efficiency.

11. **Business Process Outsourcing (BPO):** Organizations can increase efficiency by outsourcing noncore or repetitive tasks to specialized providers, allowing them to focus on their core competencies and strategic activities.

12. **Continuous Improvement (Kaizen):** Kaizen encourages a culture of continuous improvement, where employees at all levels are empowered to identify and implement small, incremental improvements in their daily work.

13. **Project Management Principles:** A body of knowledge that sets parameter for how to manage projects.

By adopting these operational methodologies, organizations can optimize their processes, reduce waste, enhance productivity, and ultimately achieve higher levels of efficiency and effectiveness in their operation. As the leader, educate yourself on the methodologies applicable to your industry and operations, enlist your high-performing team to gauge their experience with each methodology, and make a decision that will enable your team to increase output and save time. You can also create your own methodology. At AMA Consulting, we created our own way of managing contracts, executing projects, and delivering exceptional service. The AMA way is part of our brand, and it is a differentiator for us. It is unique to us, and it is an organizational protected asset. As we grow, my focus is that all our customers experience excellence, diligence, integrity, and care, regardless of the line of service we are delivering. We have created a way to make this standardization happen. When you eat McDonald's fries in Maryland, Alaska, or Paris, France, it tastes the same because McDonald's has established and matured their business over decades.

The only thing constant is change. In leading an organization, you must be prepared to navigate change and steer the ship through contingencies with your team on board and without losing the essence of the organization. This is not any easy thing to do if you have not been prepared for it. As the first one, if you have not experienced sweeping change in your organization or career yet, it is only a matter of time. The force of nature always brings about change, and in leading an organization, you must be equipped to lead through change and the chaos that comes with it. Every leader of an organization had to lead through change when the pandemic hit. The effect of the pandemic was so broad and significant that it wiped out entire industries and created new ones.

Robin Sharma, a Canadian author, motivational speaker, leadership expert, and former litigation lawyer, said, "Change is hard at first, messy in the middle, and gorgeous at the end." This certainly has been my experience as a leader and the experience of many leaders I have coached.

Why is change hard at first? Change is hard because at first, change threatens our psychological safety and harmony. We establish routines, processes, and connections to keep us safe from the danger of not being able to perform or cope with risk. Any alteration of that established norm elicits an instant negative feeling, for many reasons. The negative feeling shows up differently for each individual and the specific reasons are also different for each person. Change disrupts familiar routines, creates uncertainty, and challenges established beliefs and habits, so as the leader, you must be aware of these psychological factors and implement plans to address them when you initiate change. As a leader in an organization, you should be familiar with the change management methodologies that exist and adopt one that aligns with your organizational needs. Also realize that some methods work better for culture and process changes versus technological changes. I have outlined the most popular methodologies below. Before you review the change management methodologies, let's outline the possible types of changes that can occur in an organization:

Culture Changes: Change can occur in the organization's culture when there is new senior leadership or appetite from the workforce in the organization to adopt a new norm or do away with an old one. Culture changes take the longest time to achieve and are the hardest because they require people within an organization to change their behaviors, and this is very hard for human beings to do. Culture changes should be handled delicately and systematically for desired impact.

Technology Changes: Technology changes are the most common type of changes leaders steward, such as the use of a new software system for tracking orders or use of automation for note taking in meetings. While technology changes are common, they are also challenging because it requires people to learn something new, and this can present challenges, especially for more entrenched employees.

Reorganization and Structure Changes: Organizations going through a reorganization often bring in outside consultants because these are the most complex changes to execute. Reorganizations essentially change the makeup of an entity, sometimes even its name and overall mission. These should be done sparingly and only when absolutely necessary, but unfortunately, we see reorgs very often due to shifting policy priorities. As a consultant that has been brought in to help facilitate the change process during reorganizations in federal agencies, I can tell you that there are very few times where they are properly executed without confusion on the part of the workforce. Typically, a new leader comes in and wants to shape the organization to fit her own understanding of the mission, and everyone aligns. In these instances, it is not uncommon to see groups with mismatched functions paired together and groups with complimentary functions separated. Reorganizations have a very significant impact on the nature of the entity.

Change management methodologies are structured approaches and frameworks used to effectively plan, implement, and monitor organizational changes. These methodologies help leaders and change agents navigate the complexities of change, address resistance, and ensure successful outcomes. If you are an emerging leader and the first one, you can research these change management methodologies and see which one best suits your need, depending on the change your organization is facing. Here are some popular change management methodologies:

1. **ADKAR Model:** The ADKAR model, developed by Prosci, focuses on individual change and outlines the five building blocks of successful change: Awareness, Desire, Knowledge, Ability, and Reinforcement. It helps identify the specific steps needed to support individuals in transitioning through change.

2. **Lewin's Three-Step Model:** Developed by psychologist Kurt Lewin, this model involves three stages of change: Unfreeze, Change, and Refreeze. It emphasizes the importance of preparing individuals for change by unfreezing the current state, implementing the change, and then refreezing to make the change a permanent part of the organization's culture.

3. **Kotter's 8-Step Model:** Developed by John Kotter, this model consists of eight sequential steps to guide organizations through change: create a sense of urgency, form a powerful guiding coalition, create a vision for change, communicate the vision, empower action, generate short-term wins, consolidate gains, produce more change, and anchor new approaches in the culture.

4. **Bridges' Transition Model:** William Bridges' model focuses on the psychological and emotional aspects of change. It highlights three stages: Ending, Neutral Zone, and New Beginning. The model emphasizes the importance of acknowledging and managing the emotional impact of change to facilitate successful transitions.

5. **Agile Change Management:** This approach aligns change management practices with Agile methodologies, commonly used in project management and software development. It emphasizes collaboration, flexibility, and continuous improvement to adapt to evolving requirements and respond to change rapidly.

6. **McKinsey 7-S Model:** Though not explicitly a change management model, the McKinsey 7-S framework is often used to assess an organization's readiness for change. It analyzes seven interdependent elements: Strategy, Structure, Systems, Shared Values, Skills, Style, and Staff, to identify areas that may require adjustment to support successful change initiatives.

7. **Six Sigma:** While mainly used for process improvement, Six Sigma's DMAIC (Define, Measure, Analyze, Improve, Control) methodology can also be adapted for managing change. It

focuses on data-driven decision-making, root cause analysis, and continuous improvement to drive successful change initiatives.

8. **Prosci's Change Management Process:** Prosci's change management process combines the ADKAR model with a structured approach to guide organizations through change. It involves five phases: Prepare for change, Manage change, Reinforce change, Evaluate change, and Integrate change management into the organization's culture.

Each change management methodology brings its unique strengths and focus areas to support successful change initiatives. As mentioned earlier, the choice of methodology depends on the specific needs and context of the organization and the nature of the change being implemented. You may also combine some methodologies to address the issues you are facing with the change in your organization.

Once you have decided on your change strategy and methodology, you must weave into your activities solutions that address these psychological factors that contribute to resistance from the beginning of the change initiative.

For example, one psychological factor is fear of the unknown: In an organization, one of the most terrifying things that can happen is when word has gone out about an impending change, and people don't understand the impact of the change on them. This introduces uncertainty, and people are uncomfortable with unpredictability. Poor communication about an impending change will cause people to fear the new situation will be worse than the current one, leading to resistance, as they will cling to what they know, what's familiar, and what has proven to keep them safe. Fear of the unknown, also known as xenophobia, is a natural human emotion characterized by anxiety, discomfort, or apprehension about situations, circumstances, or experiences that are unfamiliar, uncertain, or unpredictable. It is a common psychological response to encountering something new or outside one's comfort zone.

When faced with the unknown, people may feel a sense of vulnerability and lack of control, which can trigger fear and anxiety. This fear can manifest in various ways, such as reluctance to take risks, resistance to change, avoidance of unfamiliar situations, and a strong desire to cling to the familiar and predictable. This is what your team experiences when they do not know the impact of a change before they hear its details. Oftentimes, leaders neglect to address the psychological impact of change on their people, and this is what stalls the process.

Fear of the unknown is deeply rooted in human evolution. In early human history, being cautious and wary of unfamiliar environments or potential threats was necessary for survival. While modern society has significantly reduced many life-threatening dangers, the instinctual fear response to the unknown persists in the human psyche. In the context of change management or personal growth, fear of the unknown can be a significant barrier to progress. People may resist embracing change, even if the change offers potential benefits, especially when they don't know what the benefits are or doubt the change will deliver value. As a leader initiating change, you play a critical role in overcoming this fear, which often requires building confidence, developing resilience, and reframing the unknown as an opportunity for growth and learning. Leaders must communicate effectively, provide support, and foster a positive and open environment to help individuals overcome their fear and embrace new possibilities.

Another psychological effect change has on people is loss aversion. Loss aversion is a cognitive bias that influences human decision-making and behavior. It describes the tendency of individuals to feel the impact of potential losses more profoundly than the potential gains in the same situation. The concept was first introduced in 1979 by psychologists Daniel Kahneman and Amos Tversky, in their Prospect Theory. The major loss people feel during a transition is loss of control. Often, when changes or transitions occur in an organization, only people in authority have control over what the change is, how it will be implemented, and when it will be fully operational. As a leader, you must understand that your team, without the authority to control the transition, experiences a feeling of loss.

The idea behind loss aversion is deeply rooted in human evolutionary history. Throughout our evolution, avoiding losses was crucial for survival. Losing resources, such as food or shelter, could significantly affect an individual's ability to thrive. As a result, the brain developed a heightened sensitivity to losses, making them more salient in our minds compared to potential gains. In the context of change implementation, loss aversion can play a significant role in slow or stalled adoption. When confronted with a change, whether it's in personal life or the workplace, people often face the fear of giving up something familiar, comfortable, or valued. This emotional response can lead to resistance and reluctance to embrace change.

For example, consider an organization planning to implement a new software system. Some employees may feel anxious about the change, fearing they will lose efficiency or autonomy in their work processes; they are familiar with the old system. These perceived losses can overshadow potential gains in increased productivity, streamlined operations, or improved outcomes. As a leader embarking on a change process, you must learn from your team what critical features and benefits they fear losing and target your communications around tamping down the effect of that sense of loss. You must show your team why the benefits of the new system brought on by the change is superior to the feature they will lose. Another strategy that can mitigate the effect of loss aversion is making gradual shifts instead of a one-time big change; give people time to process the new features you are bringing in with the change and let them experience the benefits before you take away the old system. Gradual and smooth transitions work better than sudden and seismic shifts. I call it a roll in and roll out approach. Always start with rolling in the new process, technology, or policy in a phased approach, and give people time to understand it, learn its benefits, and become familiar with it before you roll out the old one.

I once coached a leader who was rolling out a new telework policy. She wanted me to review the memo she had written about it to her team. It started with "Effective Immediately: Our new policy is that you have to come into the office at least twice a week."

I asked her to step back and think about her team, who had been working fully remotely for the last two years. They had gained more time because they didn't have to commute anymore, had better childcare arrangements, and saved money from not commuting. Now here comes this change, with an immediate effect: taking all that away, with no time to process it and make plans for it. I encouraged her to have a meeting with her team, letting them know the benefits of synchronous collaboration in the office twice a week and how that collaboration will save their total work hours weekly. I encouraged her to start by encouraging her team to come up with ways to shorten their work week if they worked onsite two days a week. She adopted this approach and did not get as much pushback as she anticipated. This roll in, roll out approach works. Always give people something before you take something away during a change.

Another cause of resistance to change is cognitive dissonance. Cognitive dissonance is a psychological phenomenon that occurs when individuals experience discomfort or tension due to inconsistencies between their beliefs, attitudes, or behaviors and new information or situations. The theory of cognitive dissonance was developed by psychologist Leon Festinger in the late 1950s and has since become a foundational concept in social psychology.

The essence of cognitive dissonance lies in the desire for internal consistency and the reduction of psychological discomfort. When people encounter information that challenges their existing beliefs or attitudes, they experience dissonance, which is an uncomfortable feeling of mental disharmony. This discomfort arises because holding contradictory beliefs or acting in ways that contradict personal values creates a state of cognitive conflict.

In the context of change management, cognitive dissonance plays a crucial role in understanding how individuals and organizations respond to changes in their environment, processes, or structures. When implementing significant changes, such as organizational restructurings, new technologies, or shifts in business strategies, employees and stakeholders often encounter cognitive dissonance due to the inconsistencies between the old and new ways of doing things. You must understand this as a leader. There is a natural conflict between the old and the new, especially when people feel the old better aligns with their beliefs. Be aware that introducing something new may contradict the belief systems they currently hold.

To resolve cognitive dissonance and regain psychological equilibrium, individuals typically take one of the following approaches:

Changing Beliefs or Attitudes: One way to reduce cognitive dissonance is by altering existing beliefs or attitudes to accommodate the new information. This adjustment allows individuals to create a more consistent mental framework. Leaders must know if a change requires their team to change their beliefs and attitudes and support them through that process in order to adopt the change.

Rationalization: People may attempt to rationalize conflicting information or situations to minimize the perceived inconsistency. This can involve downplaying the significance of the new information or finding alternative explanations to make it align with existing beliefs. Leaders must know that when people are rationalizing, they are not being negative; leaders must be prepared with answers to their team's questions during this rationalizing process and steer them back to the benefits of the change.

Confirmation Bias: When confronted with conflicting information, individuals may seek out or emphasize evidence that supports their existing beliefs while ignoring or discounting contradictory facts. Confirmation bias helps maintain consistency by reinforcing pre-existing views. I have seen this happen a lot in teams I've led; when people don't believe in the idea of a new initiative, they will find every evidence to prove the change is a bad idea. Leaders should be prepared for this during transitions. The best approach is to objectively weigh the evidence provided against the benefit of the change and provide a strong counter. Transitions are messy; they have crests and valleys. Leaders must have the mental agility to ride the crests and not drown in the valleys. Being prepared for objections from confirmation bias is one way to ride out a change effectively.

Scripture says, "Beware of the little foxes that spoil the vines; for our vines have tender grapes" (Song of Solomon 2:15). While psychological factors mainly affect people's attitude toward change and transitions, leaders must be aware of other peripheral things during transitions to avoid catastrophe:

GROUP NORMS AND SOCIAL INFLUENCE

People are influenced by the attitudes and behaviors of those around them. If their social circle resists change, they may be more likely to do the same to maintain group cohesion. Imagine a company that has been experiencing financial difficulties and decides to implement a significant organizational restructuring to improve efficiency and reduce costs. The change involves consolidating departments, reassigning job roles, and introducing new performance metrics, but the employee union is against the change. In this scenario, employees within the organization have established strong social connections with their colleagues over the years. They have developed a close-knit group with shared norms, attitudes, and work practices. The social cohesion within these groups can be very influential.

If the majority of employees within a particular work group or department resist the change, it can create a negative ripple effect throughout the organization due to social influence. Here's how it might unfold:

1. **Norms of Resistance:** Within certain social groups or teams, employees may collectively express resistance to the restructuring. They may have concerns about how the changes will affect their job security, workload, or work relationships.

2. **Information Sharing:** Employees within these groups tend to discuss their concerns and reinforce each other's fears and anxieties regarding the change. Information that aligns with their resistance is amplified, while positive aspects of the change are downplayed or ignored.

3. **Peer Pressure:** The employees who initially considered accepting the change might feel pressured by their social circle to join the resistance. They may fear being ostracized or rejected by their peers if they express support for the change.

4. **Emotional Contagion:** Emotions, both positive and negative, can spread within social groups. If the prevailing sentiment is resistance and negativity, it can infect others in the group, intensifying the overall resistance to change.

5. **Reduced Adoption:** As a result of the group's social influence, some employees who were initially open to the change might decide to align with the resistance group. This can hinder the overall adoption of the restructuring.

6. **Collective Action:** Social influence may even lead to collective actions, such as petitions, work slowdowns, or a decline in morale and productivity, which can further disrupt the change process.

Another small fox that can spoil a leader's tender grapes during a transition is an unexpected increase in the time and effort required to implement the change. Change often requires learning new skills and investing time and effort in the transition. The prospect of this extra work can lead to resistance. Leaders play a critical role in guiding and implementing change within an organization. However, if leaders underestimate the time and effort required for the transition process, it can have detrimental effects on the change initiative and lead to various challenges. Leaders can inadvertently undermine the transition process by underestimating its costs. The change management methodologies listed earlier can help you with strategies to mitigate these objections. I strongly encourage you as the first one to not embark on change without using a methodology that has a track record of success.

UNREALISTIC TIMELINES

Results-focused leaders often underestimate the steps required to achieve those results. Decisions on initiating change are often based on optimistic assessments, and not enough consideration is given to present deadlines, workloads, and requirements. When leaders set unrealistic timelines for the change, it puts immense pressure on employees to adapt quickly. This can lead to rushed decision-making and implementation, resulting in suboptimal outcomes. Employees may feel overwhelmed and resistant to change when they do not have enough time to adequately prepare for the transition. I have had to learn this as a leader. One thing about me is that I am very fast. I think fast, act fast, and implement fast; earlier in my leadership journey, I jumped into change fast, but I've learned that change takes time. I have developed the tact and patience to see change through. I am more realistic with the timeline for adaptation of something new within my organization. I have learned from experience.

As a leader managing a transition, do not underestimate the resources needed for the change. Change requires essential tools, training, and support for employees. Without the necessary resources, employees may struggle to acquire new skills or adapt to the change, leading to frustration and resistance. Also, do not assume employees will naturally adapt to the change without investing in comprehensive training and development programs. When employees do not receive proper training and support, they may feel ill-equipped to handle their new responsibilities, leading to resistance and decreased productivity.

Ambitious leaders are notorious for ignoring change readiness assessments. If you overlook the importance of conducting change readiness assessments to understand the organization's and employees' readiness for the change, you might not have a clear picture of potential roadblocks or areas that require additional attention and support, and you will not identify change champions who are supportive of the change and can positively influence others. If leaders fail to identify and engage these change champions, they miss an opportunity to leverage their influence in overcoming resistance and encouraging others to embrace the transition.

To avoid undermining the transition process, leaders should engage in thorough planning, conduct change readiness assessments, communicate transparently, and provide adequate resources and support for employees. They must acknowledge and address the time and effort required for change, ensure realistic timelines, and demonstrate empathy and understanding throughout the transition. By doing so, leaders can foster a more positive and supportive environment that encourages employees to embrace change, invest in learning new skills, and contribute to the organization's successful transformation. As a consultant, I have had instances where we've been brought in to conduct a change readiness assessment, and we made a recommendation that the organization should not proceed with the change at that time. Thankfully, they trusted our judgment, and two years later, the staff were able to adopt the new competency models. Had that change been forced through when we conducted the readiness assessment in the middle of the pandemic, there would have been an exodus. The truth is that the staff didn't have the appetite or stamina for such a sweeping reform of their competency models and performance metrics when they were just trying to survive the pandemic. When leading an organization, you must read the tea leaves to gauge the right time to initiate change.

9

CRISIS MANAGEMENT

Can you remember where you were when the lockdown for COVID-19 happened? Or when you got the news of 9/11? For 9/11, I was in college then and in the middle of a biology class; there was an announcement that we needed to vacate campus, as there was an active terrorist attack. It was scary and very confusing, I remember thinking, *This is the end of the world.* The dread and uncertainty were overwhelming. For COVID-19, I thought the lockdown would only last three weeks, max. Nothing prepared me for the almost one year of shut down with online school. Imagine working from home with four kids, ages two to thirteen, in online school. To say it was challenging is an understatement. Crisis can hit at any time, without warning, no matter how much you plan, cross all the Is and dot the Ts. Brian Tracy, the well-known Canadian motivational speaker, author, and personal development expert, said, "The true test of leadership is how well you function in a crisis." While crisis usually gives no notice, everything you know, believe, and have done as a leader has prepared you for it.

The first reported COVID-19 case in the United States was in January 2020. Initially, President Trump downplayed the severity of the virus, comparing it to the flu, and expressed optimism that it would disappear quickly. This was a huge mistake; as we all know, the COVID-19 pandemic became the deadliest public health crises in modern history. It resulted in millions of deaths worldwide and caused immense suffering for individuals, communities, and countries. The pandemic overwhelmed healthcare systems, led to economic hardships, disrupted education, and significantly altered daily life for billions of people. As a leader, your first response to a crisis is to assess the situation. You must quickly gather information and assess the scope and severity of the crisis. Understanding the facts and implications is essential to making informed decisions. President Trump had access to intelligence about the pandemic and information from other countries in Asia, where it originated, and Europe, where it spread, but he failed to understand what the information he was reviewing meant and its potential impact on the American people and economy.

When a crisis hits, as the leader of the organization, there are quick steps you can take to stop the bleeding and reassure your team and followers. The first is information gathering. The process begins with collecting data and information from various sources. This includes internal sources such as employees, departments, and systems, as well as external sources like media reports, government agencies, and relevant experts. The goal is to obtain a comprehensive and accurate understanding of the crisis. Information gathering is a critical and multifaceted aspect of crisis management. During a crisis, leaders and crisis management teams must gather data and information from various sources to gain a comprehensive and accurate understanding of the situation. This process should involve both internal and external sources to ensure that all relevant aspects of the crisis are considered. When a crisis hits, you the leader should request information about the crisis from all internal sources. During a crisis, leaders underestimate the value of bringing in the perspective of employees within the organization. Employees can be a valuable source of information. They might have firsthand knowledge of the crisis's impact on operations, safety, and employee well-being. Gathering feedback and insights from employees can provide a more in-depth understanding of the crisis's implications on the ground. Also, different departments within the organization might be affected differently by the crisis. Collaborating with department heads and key personnel can offer insights into specific challenges and opportunities for mitigating the impact.

One way to gather information is to leverage data from internal systems and databases that can provide crucial information about key metrics, financial implications, customer trends, supply chain disruptions, and other critical aspects relevant to the crisis. After quickly gathering information from internal sources, you should also look at external sources, monitoring media reports and coverage related to the crisis to keep a pulse on how the crisis is being perceived by the public and how it might be affecting the broader community and stakeholders.

Also, relevant government agencies might have data, guidelines, or resources related to the crisis. Staying up to date with official information from these sources can help you make better decisions and ensure compliance with regulations as you respond to the crisis.

Industry associations are another great source of information. When a crisis hits, industry-specific associations or organizations may provide valuable insights into how the crisis is affecting the sector as a whole and how other organizations are responding so you know how to position a response.

You may have to pull in experts and consultants skilled in the area the crisis is in for their perspective of the situation. Seeking input from relevant experts and consultants, such as public health experts, legal advisors, cybersecurity specialists, or crisis management professionals, can provide specialized knowledge and guidance that will save you time during a response. Take a comprehensive approach when gathering information, so you have a broader understanding of the crisis.

The different perspectives and insights from various internal and external sources can help you as the leader identify blind spots and consider potential scenarios and implications, but it's essential to verify and cross-reference information to ensure accuracy. Relying on credible sources reduces the risk of basing decisions on misinformation or rumors, which are prevalent during a crisis. The best approach is to plan for the worst but consider all possible contingencies, as opposed to having a narrow view of the crisis, only to experience a snowball effect you are not prepared for.

Another approach for gathering information during a crisis is to effect real time monitoring. Things change quickly during a crisis. In a rapidly evolving crisis, real-time monitoring of the situation is crucial. You can leverage technology and tools that provide real-time data and insights, so your decision-making and response effort is based on the most recent developments. Regular updates and communication within the crisis management team and across the organization are necessary to keep everyone informed and aligned. This is why during a crisis, you see nations set up a command center or situation room for crisis operation.

As the first one, you will probably not learn about this in your course of study or during your orientation at work until you have to manage a crisis, and at that point, it is sink or swim. I have seen people scapegoated during a crisis. Large organizations and bureaucracies are notorious for identifying someone to take the fall during a crisis so that they can demonstrate to their shareholders/stakeholders that they handled the crisis; inexperienced leaders are usually the ones who take that fall. So these tips will help you be prepared, should a crisis hit.

Lastly, as you gather information, it is best to establish a centralized information hub. Creating a centralized repository or information hub can streamline data collection and access. Having a single source of truth facilitates collaboration and ensures that everyone involved has access to the most current and relevant information. Leaders must cast a wide net and draw on various sources of information to develop a clear and informed picture of the crisis's scope and severity. A well-informed understanding of the crisis enables effective decision-making, communication, and strategic planning, positioning the organization to navigate the challenges and emerge stronger from the crisis.

Once you establish a process for gathering information during a crisis, the next thing you must do as a leader is to tease out the facts from the information you have gathered. During a crisis, the people you lead and the customers you serve have one primary emotion: fear. Your response should build trust in their minds and reassure them that your response will avert the crisis and protect their interests. Ensuring facts and accuracy in crisis management is of utmost importance. Making decisions based on unreliable or false data can lead to misguided actions, exacerbate the crisis, and erode trust in leadership. Crises often generate a flood of information from various sources, including social media, news outlets, and hearsay. Some of this information may be inaccurate, misleading, or based on rumors. Leaders must exercise caution and critically evaluate the credibility of sources before accepting information as facts. Accurate information forms the foundation for effective decision-making.

I recently watched the movie *To Catch a Killer,* about the inner workings of the CIA, FBI, and local law enforcement to catch a serial killer. The movie was set in Baltimore, Maryland; in the movie, the head of command was often at loggerheads with senior leaders at FBI headquarters; the FBI wanted more information to be released to the public and wanted to enlist the public's help to catch the killer, but the head of the operation didn't want that because he felt it would inhibit them from getting actual leads to the true suspect. The head of the operation was right. As soon as the public was brought into the investigation, various people started insinuating they were the killer, and it led to unnecessary deaths of innocent people. Talk about a crisis on top of a crisis.

You need reliable data and evidence to understand the situation fully and devise appropriate response strategies. Decisions based on fact are more likely to be effective and successful in mitigating the crisis's impact. Inaccurate or exaggerated information can fuel panic and fear among employees, stakeholders, and the public. Leaders must strive to provide accurate and trustworthy information to maintain calm, instill confidence, and prevent unnecessary anxiety. Leaders who prioritize facts and accuracy in their communications build trust and credibility with their teams and stakeholders. When people trust their leaders to provide accurate information, they are more likely to follow guidance and instructions during a crisis. If you were in a trust deficit with your team before the crisis, you need to make an extra effort to ensure you are considering accurate information before acting.

When a crisis hits, you have various voices in your ears; however, the responsibility to verify the authenticity and credibility of your sources is yours. Use your intuition, past experiences, domain expertise, and network to vet the information you receive. Relying on verified sources, such as government agencies, reputable news organizations, and subject matter experts, reduces the risk of spreading misinformation. Another quick tool to vet information is cross-referencing information from multiple sources to validate its accuracy. If multiple credible sources report the same information, it is more likely to be reliable and true.

From the get-go, set the intention to be transparent and honest in your communication. If you do not have all the answers, it is better to admit it and commit to providing updates as soon as more information becomes available. Being transparent about the challenges and uncertainties can enhance credibility. Crises can give rise to rumors and false narratives. Leaders should be proactive in addressing misinformation and countering false narratives with accurate information. Ensuring facts and accuracy in crisis management is essential for making well-informed decisions, maintaining trust and credibility, and effectively navigating the challenges of a crisis. Leaders must be diligent in verifying information, communicating transparently, and relying on credible sources to provide accurate guidance during uncertain and challenging times.

After you have vetted the information you gather during a crisis, you should understand the nature of the crisis. For example, the COVID-19 pandemic was a public health crisis that morphed into a public health and economic crisis due to the lockdown. Different crises require different responses. Leaders must determine the type of crisis they are dealing with, such as a natural disaster, cyber-attack, financial crisis, public health emergency, or reputational crisis. Each type of crisis presents unique challenges and requires specific expertise and strategies. As a leader, you should also assess the extent to which the crisis has affected (or may potentially affect) your organization and other auxiliary organizations. This involves understanding the geographical spread, the number of people involved, and the potential consequences on operations, finances, reputation, and safety. The COVID-19 pandemic was gigantic, and its effects were multidimensional. Beyond the health impact, the pandemic had wide-ranging consequences on economies, mental health, education, and more. Leaders needed to adopt a comprehensive approach that addressed these multifaceted effects of crisis that have multidimensional effects.

During a crisis response, you as the leader may have to balance some polarities, as a response to curtail negative effects in one area may elicit a negative consequence in another area. For example, the pandemic highlighted the delicate balance between protecting public health and maintaining economic stability. Leaders had to make difficult decisions about when and how to implement restrictions to curb the virus's spread while considering the economic well-being of their communities. Dr. Max McKeown is a British author, speaker, and strategic adviser known for his work in the fields of innovation, leadership, and strategy; he said, "Adaptability is about the powerful difference between adapting to cope and adapting to win." His book, *Adaptability: The Art of Winning in an Age of Uncertainty* introduces the concept of the Adaptability Quotient (AQ), which measures an individual's or organization's readiness to adapt and thrive in changing circumstances. He discusses the components that contribute to a high AQ, including flexibility, resilience, and a willingness to experiment. I agree with most of the tenets he proposes; very rigid, structured leaders and organizations struggle more during a crisis because of tunnel vision. During a crisis, your peripheral vision should be sharp to properly ascertain the nature of the crisis, respond effectively, and emerge better. During a crisis, you should not just aim to cope, but win when the dust settles.

The Monica Lewinsky scandal was a major political and public relations crisis that unfolded in the late 1990s, involving President Bill Clinton and Monica Lewinsky, a White House intern. The scandal revolved around allegations of a sexual relationship between Clinton and Lewinsky during Clinton's time in office. Poor crisis communication exacerbated the situation and intensified the scandal. I will use this story to illustrate how poor communication (actually a lie) turned a crisis into a political tsunami that is entrenched in history.

AFFAIR AND ALLEGATIONS

Monica Lewinsky, a young intern at the White House, allegedly engaged in a sexual relationship with President Bill Clinton. The affair took place between 1995 and 1997 but came to light in 1998, when Lewinsky confided in a coworker, Linda Tripp, who secretly recorded their conversations. Linda Tripp shared the recordings with independent counsel Kenneth Starr, who was investigating other allegations against President Clinton. As a result, the affair was exposed to the public and became a national scandal. President Clinton initially denied the allegations. The initial response by the Clinton administration was to deny the intern's claim and portray Lewinsky as a liar. This approach aimed to contain the scandal but ultimately led to a lack of transparency and credibility.

President Clinton's public statements were inconsistent, creating confusion and raising suspicions. He famously stated, "I did not have sexual relations with that woman, Miss Lewinsky," which later proved to be untrue. The scandal tarnished President Clinton's reputation and distracted from his policy agenda. It also drew significant media attention and public scrutiny. The US public was split on their feelings about the scandal. People on the left felt the scandal was a personal failure that didn't need to affect the president's job approval ratings and saw the impeachment as a witch hunt, while those on the right felt it was a defining factor of his presidency worthy of impeachment due to his poor judgment and lack of candor under oath. I believe the president's communications team did everything you should not do when responding to a crisis.

The initial strategy of denying the allegations and portraying Lewinsky as untrustworthy undermined the credibility of the administration. The denial was contradicted by later revelations and evidence. This is why leaders must quickly gather all the facts about a crisis, vet the data, and properly qualify what exactly they are dealing with early on; your adversaries are waiting for the day of crisis to exploit the situation and nail you. If the administration knew there was evidence available contrary to their position and still denied it, it was not smart. It made matters worse. The truth will always come out. When a crisis hits, surround yourself with people who will give you the facts so you can prepare the best response and limit the opening for bad actors to exploit the crisis.

President Clinton's lack of transparency and evasive answers eroded public trust. The inconsistent statements he made further fueled suspicions and damaged his credibility. Crisis communications must be as transparent as possible. Most times, when there is a public crisis, leaders must come out to give press statements and answer questions. As an emerging leader, if you ever find yourself on this hot seat, please prepare and practice. A lack of transparency only leads to suspicion. Prepare your succinct points to share, stick to the facts, and avoid speculation; if you don't have the answers, admit it and follow up with details later. Also, pay attention to your language and emotions. Realize all eyes are on you, and people are not only listening to what you say, they are reading the meaning behind your words in your body language. Admit wrong or error fast, without exposing yourself to unnecessary liabilities; talk to the experts and be aware. Try not to make absolute statements you may have to take back. President Clinton eventually admitted to the affair after the evidence became overwhelming. The delay in acknowledging the truth contributed to the perception of dishonesty and manipulation.

Another mistake the president's team made was to focus on legal technicalities. They focused heavily on legal technicalities, such as the definition of "sexual relations," rather than addressing the broader ethical and moral implications of the situation. They failed to see the crisis the president faced was a breach of trust of the people and a fall from moral standing, not an infraction of the law. The crisis was not a matter of law. It was a matter of a man cheating on his wife with the secretary; it was about a man with power exploiting a young woman because he could. It was about the exposure of the shortcomings of an otherwise very powerful and charismatic authority figure. During crisis communication, keep the main thing the main thing and respond to that; avoid trying to win the argument on a technicality. It never works because during a crisis, people are very alert and tuned in, and there is so much information swirling around, so the technicality gets lost in the conversation. In the Lewinsky scandal, the crisis response did not effectively address the emotional and moral aspects of the scandal, leading to public perception that the administration was more concerned with political survival than taking responsibility. The poor crisis communication strategy in the Monica Lewinsky scandal, characterized by denial, deception, and lack of transparency, exacerbated the crisis and eroded trust in the administration. The focus on legal maneuvering and technicalities detracted from addressing the ethical and moral dimensions of the situation. The lessons learned from this crisis highlight the importance of transparency, honesty, and a comprehensive crisis communication approach that addresses both legal and ethical aspects.

CONCLUSION

Leadership is hard. No matter how much you prepare, there will be moments of adversity that will almost crush you. Being the first one is more challenging because you are the trailblazer; no one has walked this path before you, so you have to endure the pricks and stings of plants on the path you are blazing. However, success in leadership is possible. You can achieve your goal, you can build that business, you can lead that team to great heights, you can usher in change, and you can survive that storm. It starts with you, the leader, the instrument. Be intentional about continuing to feed, nurture, and grow your body, soul, and spirit. Your innate personality is set, but how you use your mind to act it out is up to you. Your biological makeup is what you got, but how you use your temple is up to you. As a leader, self-care and management is a responsibility you must not neglect. Leaders are notorious for taking care of everyone and abandoning themselves. This is irresponsible. I had to learn this the hard way. In 2020, I suffered a severe breakdown from burnout and stress. I thought I was going to die; while I was in that dark state of indescribable fatigue, depression, and anxiety, I wondered what God would say to me if I went to heaven. I knew He would scold me for not taking care of the gifts He deposited in me and living carelessly. I knew He would reprimand me for not achieving the purpose for which He sent me and seeking the validation of people instead.

The truth is, I was not living with wisdom. I was trying so hard to be everything to everybody. I knew my values, gifts, and talents, but I felt they were not enough, so I constantly stretched myself outside my calling and strength field to prove my worth, I didn't rest, didn't exercise, and certainly didn't eat right. I had no boundaries with people and didn't even know that I could pick my own people, people who aligned with my values, and so I was constantly being betrayed. I somehow always ended up in misfit relationships. Until I started therapy and started to work through some of the tenets I shared in the book, I didn't experience wholeness and joy. Even when I was effective and financially successful, I was not well. I learnt that you cannot progress beyond your level of wellness. As you read through the points in this book on self-leadership, remember to be kind to yourself; understand that you will continue to grow and master yourself all your life. Give yourself grace. Here are some practices that can help you on the journey to accepting your identity, growing your capacity, and sharpening your vision as a leader:

TIPS TO INCREASE COMPETENCIES OF LEADING YOURSELF

Self-Care

1. **Prioritize Sleep and Rest:** Adequate sleep is crucial for cognitive function, decision-making, and overall well-being. Aim for seven to nine hours of quality sleep each night. Take breaks, and give

yourself white space to avoid the habit of cramming your schedule with no days off.

2. **Follow Healthy Nutrition:** Fuel your body with nutritious foods that provide sustained energy. Know what foods are good for you, and create a boundary for yourself to stick to them.

3. **Exercise Regularly:** Engage in regular physical activity to reduce stress, improve mood, and enhance overall health.

4. **Practice Mindfulness and Meditation:** Practice mindfulness techniques or meditation to reduce stress and enhance focus. Even a few minutes of deep breathing can have a positive impact.

5. **Take Time for Hobbies:** Dedicate time to activities you enjoy outside of work to relax and recharge; this sparks creativity and keeps you refreshed.

6. **Set Boundaries:** Establish clear boundaries between work and personal life to prevent burnout. Disconnect from work-related tasks during off-hours.

7. **Develop Social Support:** Maintain connections with friends, family, and peers who provide emotional support and a sense of community.

8. **Take Time for Self-Reflection:** Regularly assess your well-being and stress levels. Adjust your routine as needed to maintain balance. Use a journal to keep a record of your insights and growth.

9. **Celebrate Your Wins:** Get in the habit of celebrating yourself, and ditch the fake humility mindset. It is not easy to be you.

Time Management

1. **Prioritize Tasks:** Identify the most important tasks and focus on those first. Use techniques like the Eisenhower Matrix to prioritize effectively.

2. **Delegate:** Delegate tasks to team members based on their strengths and expertise. This empowers your team and allows you to focus on strategic matters.

3. **Effective Planning:** Plan your day, week, and month in advance. Set realistic goals and allocate time for both work and self-care.

4. **Limit Multitasking:** Focus on one task at a time to enhance productivity and reduce stress.

5. **Time Blocking:** Allocate specific time blocks for different tasks to stay organized and prevent constant task-switching.

6. **Learn to Say No:** Assess your commitments and avoid overloading yourself. Politely decline tasks that are beyond your capacity.

Stress Management

1. **Practice Problem-Solving:** Address challenges methodically, and seek solutions. Break down complex problems into manageable steps.

2. **Effective Communication:** Foster open communication with your team to prevent misunderstandings and conflicts that can contribute to stress.

3. **Flexibility:** Embrace change and adapt to unexpected developments. Cultivate a mindset of resilience and agility.

4. **Avoid negativity and negative triggers:** Remove negativity and negative triggers from your immediate environment. You may not be able to control all environments, but make your immediate area suitable for you.

5. **Celebrate Achievements:** Acknowledge and celebrate milestones and achievements, both big and small, to boost morale.

6. **Seek Support:** If you're feeling overwhelmed, don't hesitate to seek guidance from mentors, coaches, or counselors.

7. **Take Breaks:** Regular short breaks throughout the day can help you recharge and maintain focus.

8. **Seek medical and mental health treatment:** If you have a medical condition, stay diligent with your prescribed treatment regimen, and keep well. If you've experienced severe trauma, get help and heal.

TIPS TO INCREASE COMPETENCIES ON LEADING PEOPLE

When it comes to leading people, remember two things: (1) Human beings are your best resource and will cause you the most pain. (2) You can and should pick your people. You are not for everyone. Always do your best to affect people positively and leave people better than you met them. See everyone you encounter first as a human being who is worthy of dignity and respect. Also know that leadership is lonely and painful because people are flawed, imperfect, and sometimes, wicked. If you invest in learning how to identify people who align with your values, have the capacity you need, and are willing to come on board with your vision, and you have what they need in return, the pain and loneliness that come with leadership will be lessened. In your leadership journey, understand that you can pick your people, and people can pick their people too; you may not be their person. Respect the genius that lies in every human being, but do not make another human being the source of validation of your worth. Simply put, no one else was designed to do that for you.

Leading people can sometimes be accompanied by feelings of loneliness and even instances of betrayal. Here are ten tips to help you thrive despite these challenges:

1. **Cultivate Self-Awareness:** Understand your emotions, strengths, and limitations. Self-awareness enables you to navigate challenges more effectively and seek support when needed.
2. **Build a Support Network:** Connect with fellow leaders, mentors, or colleagues who understand the demands of leadership. Sharing experiences and seeking advice can help alleviate feelings of loneliness.
3. **Focus on Purpose:** Remind yourself of the larger purpose of your leadership role. Keeping your mission and goals in mind can provide motivation and fulfillment.
4. **Practice Resilience:** Develop resilience to bounce back from setbacks and betrayal. Focus on your ability to adapt, learn, and grow from challenging experiences.
5. **Communicate Openly:** Foster transparent and open communication to the appropriate measure with your team. When you're vulnerable about your feelings, it can create a more supportive environment.

6. **Set Realistic Expectations:** Understand that not everyone will support your decisions, and betrayal may occur. Set realistic expectations for yourself and others to manage disappointments.

7. **Enjoy Your Own Company, and Be Happy Now:** Sit with yourself, and enjoy your self-conversations and thoughts. It can be very refreshing; do not delay your happiness. Don't fall into the habit of "I'll be happy when …"

8. **Focus on Positive Relationships:** Nurture relationships with those who offer genuine support and positivity. Surrounding yourself with uplifting people can counterbalance negative experiences.

9. **Seek Professional Help:** A good leader should have a therapist, coach, or spiritual guide. I have all three. Professional support can provide valuable strategies to cope and thrive.

Remember that leadership can be challenging, but it also offers opportunities for growth, impact, and personal development. By adopting these strategies, you can enhance your resilience, well-being, and overall ability to thrive, despite the challenges that may arise.

TIPS TO INCREASING COMPETENCIES ON LEADING AN ORGANIZATION

At some point, you must lead in a system or organization that is a separate entity from you. Understand that organizations are complex and very nuanced, and you must master these unique complexities and nuances to be successful. Understand that the system in an organization can torpedo your team goals and derail your focus. To lead an organization, you must be comfortable in gray areas, confident in ambiguity, and familiar with change.

1. **Study the Organizational Landscape:** Commit to continuously understand the organizational structure, culture, and dynamics. Learn about key stakeholders, decision-makers, and informal power structures.

2. **Build Relationships:** Cultivate strong relationships with colleagues, team members, and stakeholders. Solid relationships are the highest currency when leading organizations.

3. **Adaptability:** Embrace change and uncertainty as a constant in organizational life. Develop the ability to pivot and adjust strategies in response to evolving situations.

4. **Strategic Thinking:** Apply a strategic mindset to align your team's goals with the broader organizational objectives. Understand how your work fits into the bigger picture.

5. **Negotiation Skills:** Develop strong negotiation and influencing skills to navigate competing interests and secure resources for your team.

6. **Political Awareness:** Be attuned to organizational politics without compromising your values. Navigate delicate situations and conflicts with sensitivity and discretion.

7. **Communication Mastery:** Hone your communication skills to convey complex ideas clearly and persuasively. Tailor your message to different audiences, and foster open dialogue.

8. **Embrace Ambiguity:** Thrive in uncertain situations by remaining adaptable and making informed decisions, despite incomplete information.

9. **Problem-Solving Skills:** Develop robust problem-solving skills to address challenges and roadblocks that may arise within the organization.

10. **Master Polarity Management:** In very large organizations, a lot of issues are not problems that can be solved but polarities that must be managed. Understand that distinction, and keep the poles balanced.

11. **Lead by Example:** Demonstrate the values and behaviors you expect from your team. Your leadership style sets the tone for the work culture and influences others.

Remember, leading within a complex organization requires patience, persistence, and continuous learning. By mastering these skills and strategies, you can navigate the nuanced landscape of the organization and lead your team to success, no matter what challenges arise.

I hope that at this point, you are experiencing some relief: relief from knowing you are not alone, and your experiences as the first one is more common than you know. I hope you have clarity on who you are as a leader, what you are called to do on the earth, and who your people are that will help you accomplish your purpose. I hope you now have the confidence to take up space and lead because you know what to do, and you are sure you are on the right path. I am rooting for you. I am cheering you on. I am right beside you, and I know you will win. A magnificent leader is one who shines their light so bright they light the path of others. I want you to win because when you do, you will shine your light for others too, and they will shine their light for others too, and that's how we do great things in the world.

Printed in the United States
by Baker & Taylor Publisher Services